F. W. (Frederic William) Farrar

An essay on the origin of language, based on modern researches

F. W. (Frederic William) Farrar

An essay on the origin of language, based on modern researches

ISBN/EAN: 9783741157479

Manufactured in Europe, USA, Canada, Australia, Japa

Cover: Foto ©Thomas Meinert / pixelio.de

Manufactured and distributed by brebook publishing software
(www.brebook.com)

F. W. (Frederic William) Farrar

An essay on the origin of language, based on modern researches

AN ESSAY

ON THE

ORIGIN OF LANGUAGE.

Note on p 84 of some earlier English owner. So, p. 105.

A work written under the fascination of Renan & Bunsen & Jowett: & giving, unhappily, too little heed to the statements of Genesis, as to man's origin, the descent from Noah's three sons, & the confusion of Tongues at Babel

AN ESSAY

ON THE

ORIGIN OF LANGUAGE,

BASED ON MODERN RESEARCHES,

AND ESPECIALLY ON THE WORKS OF M. RENAN.

BY FREDERIC W. FARRAR, M.A.

LATE FELLOW OF TRINITY COLLEGE, CAMBRIDGE.

LONDON:
JOHN MURRAY, ALBEMARLE STREET.
1860.

Vide. on f 8 ff. of some earlier English ones. So, f. 105.
A work written under the fascination of Renan
& Bunsen & Jowett : & gives, unhappily, too
little heed to the statements of Genesis, as to
man's origin, the descent from Noah's three
sons, & the confusion of Tongues at Babel.

TO

RICHARD GARNETT, ESQ.,

OF THE BRITISH MUSEUM,

.

These Pages are Dedicated,

IN

REMEMBRANCE OF MANY ACTS OF HELP AND KINDNESS.

.

PREFACE.

I wish this little book to be in every respect as unpretending as possible. I do not presume to represent myself as an original investigator, nor do I aspire to a greater distinction than that of representing clearly and intelligently the views of those distinguished writers who have made the study of philology the chief pursuit of their lives.

While I have quoted my authorities for almost every statement of importance, I have generally used my own language, and even in those paragraphs which I have put between inverted commas I have so frequently abbreviated, expanded, or transposed, that the pas-

sages must not be criticised as though they
had been intended for direct translations.

•   I do not think that I have ever borrowed from
any writer, English, French, or German, without
ample acknowledgment. I would not be so
dishonest as to shine in borrowed plumes. If
in one or two cases I have been guilty of
apparent plagiarism it is certainly only from
the works of those authors whom I cannot be
considered to • have robbed wilfully, because
their writings are honourably referred to on
almost every page. I wish this remark to
apply especially to the very clear, learned, and
beautiful treatises of M. Ernest Renan, to which
I am largely indebted, and without which I
should not have undertaken this work.

The questions here handled have always been
to me full of interest; and these chapters have
been chiefly written because I have invariably
found that they are also full of interest to young
learners. Should it be proved that I have rashly

intruded on a task beyond my powers, no one will more regret this attempt than I shall myself.

The books of which I have made *chief* use in the following pages are

Grimm, *Ueber den Ursprung der Sprache.*
Heyse, *System der Sprachwissenschaft.*
Lersch, *Die Sprachphilosophie der Alten.*
Renan, *De l'Origine du Langage.*
Renan, *Histoire Générale des Langues Sémitiques.*
Charma, *Essai sur le Langage.*
Nodier, *Notions de Linguistique.*
Bunsen, *Philosophy of Universal History.*
Max Müller, *Survey of Languages.*
Pictet, *Les Origines Indo-Européennes.*
Garnett's *Philological Essays.*
Dr. Donaldson's *Cratylus,* and *Varronianus.*

It need scarcely be said, however, that I have read and consulted very many besides these, and indeed every book that I could obtain which seemed to bear directly upon the subject.

I will only add with M. Nodier—"J'ai écrit

sur la Linguistique, parce que je ne connois aucun livre qui renferme les notions principales d'une manière claire, sous une forme accessible aux esprits simples, qui ne soit pas repoussante pour les esprits délicats."

FALMOUTH,
Aug., 1860.

CONTENTS.

CHAPTER I.

THE ORIGIN OF LANGUAGE.

PAGE

THE faculty of speech.—Definition of language.—Importance of philology.—Three main theories on the origin of language—1. That language was innate and organic.—Curious errors.—Objections to this view.—2. That language was the result of imitation and convention.—Objections.—3. That language was revealed.—In what sense this may be held to be true.—The phrase obscure, and leads to many misconceptions.—Danger of a misapplied literalism.—Five objections to the common belief.—The real meaning of Gen. ii. 19, 20.—Rightly understood it exactly accords with the true theory.—Germ of truth in each of these views.   1

CHAPTER II.

THE PSYCHOLOGICAL DEVELOPMENT OF THE IDEA OF SPEECH.

GERMINAL development of language.—How came words to be accepted as signs ?—The inquiry not absurd.—What is a word ?—Words only express the relations of things.—Connection of thought and speech.—Growth of individuality.—Theory of M. Steinthal.—Speech depends on the power of abstraction; the transformation of intuitions into ideas. — 1. Impressions awoke sounds.-

PAGE

2. Sounds, by the association of ideas, recalled impressions.—3. Sounds became words by connecting the external object and the inward impression.—Influence of organism.—Earliest impressions expressed by the simplest sounds.—Influence of women.—Influences of climate. 34

CHAPTER III.

THE LAWS OF SPECIAL SIGNIFICANCE, OR THE CREATION OF ROOTS.

WORDS never *purely* arbitrary.—They *become* conventional in time.—Corruptions produced by the dislike of mechanical words.—Inappropriate corruptions.—Words, significant at first, are allowed to become conventional.—Grammar the *life* of a language.—Onomatopœic or *imitative* words. —*Motive* of words.—Delicacy of the appellative faculty. —The imitation always purely artistic.—Instances of the spontaneous tact which gives rise to new names. . . 53

CHAPTER IV.

ONOMATOPŒIA.

SOUNDS naturally used as the signs of sounds; as among infants, and savage races.—Wide application of this law overlooked.—The imitation modified organically and ideally.—Admirable perfection of the organs of sound.— Boundless capabilities of language.—Diversity of *relations* gave rise to different imitations.—Roots universally onomatopœic.—Cause of dialectic variety.—Interjections and onomatopœia the two natural elements of language.— Instances of words derived from exclamations; and from imitation.—Supposed vulgarity of onomatopœic words.— Their real dignity when well used.—Instances from the poets.—They cannot be avoided.—Harmonies of language. 72

CHAPTER V.

THE DEVELOPMENT OF ROOTS.

PAGE

Roots supposed to be primitive and irreducible. — Words derived from sensible images ; the personal pronouns ; and even the numerals.—The verb 'to be,' in all languages, from a material root.—Permutations and combinations of a few roots.—Instances of their diffusiveness. The root 'ach.'—The root 'dhu.'—The same root to express opposite meanings.—Roots refracted and reflected.—Important applications of these remarks.   . 97

CHAPTER VI.

METAPHOR.

We know nothing absolutely.—Language an asymptote.— Necessity of analogy to express things.—All words ultimately derivable from sensible ideas.—Instances in the Semitic languages.—Graphic effects thus produced.— Words involve all history.—Catachresis and metaphor.— Defence of both from the charge of imperfection.— Necessity, power, and value of metaphor.—Comparisons of style.—Rigid accuracy and clumsiness of scientific terminology.—Words are but symbols.—The two worlds. —Poetry of life to the primal man, and its influence on language.—A nation's language expresses its character. . 110

CHAPTER VII.

WORDS NOTHING IN THEMSELVES.

Inferences drawn from the derivation of all words from 'sensible ideas.'—Gradual degeneracy of the Sensational School.—Condillac.—Helvetius.—The Diversions of Purley.—Real derivation of the words 'If' and 'Truth.' —What words really stand for.—The conclusions of nominalism need not be accepted.—Reason.—Words which can only be explained by the idea.   .   .   . 147

CHAPTER VIII.

THE LAWS OF PROGRESS IN LANGUAGE.

PAGE

THESE laws psychological. — 1. Languages advance from
exuberance to moderation by eliminating superfluities.—
Unity of speech the result of civilisation.—Redundancy
marks an early stage of thought.—Superfluous words
dropped or desynonymised.—2. Languages advance from
indetermination to grammar.—Simplicity succeeds complexity.—Instances of agglutination.—3. Languages advance from synthesis to analysis. — Tmesis a relic of
Polysynthetism.—Analysis not inferior to synthesis for
the expression of thought.—Instances in the Indo-
European and Semitic languages.—Grimm on the English
language.—Some would add a 4th law, viz.: the progress
from monosyllabism.—Arguments in favour of this law.
— It remains very questionable; only a convenient
hypothesis.　.　.　.　.　.　.　.　. 166

CHAPTER IX.

THE FAMILIES OF LANGUAGES.

STAGES of Language.—The logical order not the historical.—
1. The Indo-European and Arian family.—Its unity and
importance.—Life of the early Arians.—" Linguistic
Palæontology."—2. The Semitic family.—Its character
and divisions. — 3. The Allophylian or Turanian (?)
family (?).—Can only be called a 'family' hypothetically.
—Includes a vast number of languages, which have *very
little* connection with each other.　.　.　.　. 185

CHAPTER X.

ARE THERE ANY PROOFS OF A SINGLE PRIMITIVE LANGUAGE?

IMMENSE number of languages dead as well as living.—
Three irreducible families.—Arguments in favour of an
original language. —1. All may be derived (not from

PAGE

each other, but) from some lost language.—Objections.—
2. Supposed affinities between different families. i. Non-
Sanskritic elements in Celtic. ii. Possible reduction of
the triliteral Semitic roots.—Objections.—3. Languages
apparently anomalous. — Egyptian, Berber, &c.— How
they may possibly be accounted for. — Inference. —
Apparent successions of races.—1. The inferior races.—
2. The semi-civilised.—3. The great noble races . . 203

CHAPTER XI.

THE FUTURE OF LANGUAGE.

1. Destinies of the Arian race.—The future of the English
language.—The distinction of nations a design of Providence.—2. Advantages which result from diversities of
language.—Indispensable for the preservation of truth.—
Value of knowing languages.—3. A universal language
could, in the present state of the world, only last for a
short time.—Conclusion. 220

A LIST of books valuable as forming an Introduction to the
Study of Philology. 229

AN ESSAY

ON

THE ORIGIN OF LANGUAGE.

CHAPTER I.

THE ORIGIN OF LANGUAGE.

"Sprache ist der volle Athem menschlicher Seele."—GRIMM.

OF all the faculties wherewith God has endowed his noblest creature, none is more divine and mysterious than the faculty of speech. It is the gift whereby man is raised above the beasts; the gift whereby soul speaks to soul; the gift whereby mere pulses of articulated air become breathing thoughts and burning words; the gift whereby we understand the affections of men and give expression to the worship of God; the gift whereby the lip of divine * inspiration uttering things simple and unperfumed and unadorned, reacheth

* Σίβυλλα δὲ μαινομένῳ στόματι καθ' Ἡράκλειτον ἀγέλαστα καὶ ἀκαλλώπιστα καὶ ἀμύριστα φθεγγομένη χιλίων ἐτῶν ἐξικνεῖται τῇ φωνῇ διὰ τὸν θεόν.—Plut. de Pyth. Orac. p. 397 et p. 627. Wytt. Lapalle's *Heraclitus*, p. 29.

B

with its passionate voice through a thousand generations by the help of God.

Language is the sum total of those articulate
sounds which man, by the aid of this marvellous
faculty of speech, has produced and accepted as the
signs of all those inward and outward phenomena
wherewith he is made acquainted by sense and
thought. These signs are "those* shadows of
the soul, those living sounds which we call words!
and compared with them how poor are all other
monuments of human power, or perseverance, or
skill, or genius! They render the mere clown an
artist, nations immortal, writers, poets, philosophers divine!" Let him who would rightly understand the grandeur and dignity of speech,
meditate on the deep mystery involved in the
revelation of the Lord Jesus as the Word of God.

No study is more rich in grand results than the
study of language, and to no study can we look
with greater certainty to elucidate the earliest
history of mankind. For the roots of language †

---

* Sir John Stoddart. "Bei allem was Sprache heissen soll,
wird schlechterdings nichts weiter beabsichtiget, als die Bezeichnung des Gedankens."—Fichte, *Von der Sprachfähigkeit und
dem Ursprunge der Sprache.* "Die Sprache ist die Aeusserung
des denkenden Geistes in articulirten Lauten."—Heyse, *System der
Sprachwissenschaft,* S. 35.

† Grimm, *über den Ursprung der Sprache,* S. 11.

spring in the primitive liberty of human intelligence, and therefore its records bear on them the
traces of human history. We read with deep
interest the works of individual genius, and trace
in them the life and character of the men on
whom it has been bestowed ; we toilfully examine
the unburied monuments of extinct nations, and
are rewarded for years of labour if we can finally
succeed in gaining a feeble glimpse of their history
by deciphering the unknown letters carved on the
crumbling fragments of half-calcined stone; but
in language we have the history not only of indi-
viduals but of nations ; not only of nations but of
mankind. For unlike music and poetry, which
are the special privilege of the few, language * is
the property of all, as necessary and accessible as
the air we breathe. Of all that men have invented
and combined ; of all that they have produced or
interchanged among themselves ; of all that they
have drawn from their peculiar organism, language is the noblest and most indispensible trea-
sure. An immediate emanation of human nature,
and progressing with it, language is the common
blessing, the common patrimony, of mankind. It
is an † admirable poem on the history of all ages;

* Grimm, s. 52.
† Renan, *De l'Origine du Langage.* Deux. éd. p. 69.

a living monument, on which is written the
genesis of human thought. Thus " the ground *
on which our civilisation stands is a sacred one,
for it is the deposit of thought. For language,
as it is the mirror, so is it the product of reason,
and as it embodies thought, so is it the child of
thought. In it are deposited the primordial
sparks of that celestial fire, which, from a once
bright centre of civilisation, has streamed forth
over the inhabited earth, and which now already,
after less than three myriads of years, forms a
galaxy round the globe, a chain of light from pole
to pole."

Philology, the science which devotes itself to
the study of language, has recently† arrived at
results almost undreamed of by preceding centuries. Indeed, it received its most vigorous im-
pulse from the acquaintance with the languages
of India, and, above all, with Sanskrit, which,
like so many other great blessings, directly resulted from our dominion in India. Already it
has thrown new light on many of the most per-
plexing problems of religion, history, and ethno-
graphy ; and, being yet but an infant science, it
is in all probability destined to achieve triumphs,

* Bunsen *on the Philosophy of Universal History*, ii. 126.
† Humboldt's *Cosmos*, ii. 107—109, ed. Sabine.

of which at present we can but dimly prophesy the consequences.[*]

Since the most ancient monuments of Sanskrit, Zend,[†] Hebrew, and in fact of all languages, are separated, perhaps by thousands of years from [†] the appearance of language (*i. e.*, from the creation of the human race), it might seem impossible to throw any light on that most interesting of all considerations, the *origin* of language. And yet so permanent are the creations of speech, so invariable and ascertainable are the laws of its mutation, that the geologist is less clearly able to describe the convulsions of the earth's strata than the philologist to point out, by the indications of language, the undoubted traces of a

[*] Philology has been well defined as the cognitio cogniti, and Comparative Grammar, (the branch of Philology which occupies itself with the study of the birth, the development, and the decadence of various languages, together with their divergences and affinities), has deserved the title of Θριγκὸς μαθημάτων φιλολογικῶν, "the coping-stone of philological inquiries." See *Science Comparative des Langues*, par Louis Benloew. Paris, 1858.

[†] Thus, though Zend and Sanskrit are the oldest languages of the Indo-European family, they are offsets of an *older* primitive one. "Among other evidences of this, may be mentioned the changes that words had already undergone in Zend and Sanscrit from the original form they had in the parent tongue; as in the number 'twenty,' which being in the Zend '*visaiti*,' and in Sanscrit '*vinsaiti*,' shews that they have thrown off the 'd' of the original 'dva,' two."—Sir G. Wilkinson in Rawlinson's *Herod.* i. p. 280.

nation's previous life. On the stone tablets of
the universe, God's own finger has written the
changes which millions of years have wrought on
the mountain and the plain; in the fluid air,
which he articulates into human utterance, man
has preserved for ever the main facts of his past
history, and the main processes of his inmost
soul. The sonorous wave, indeed, which transmits
to our ears the uttered thought, reaches but a
little distance, and then vanishes like the tremu-
lous ripple on the surface of the sea; but, conscious of his destiny, man invented writing to
give it perpetuity from age to age. Its short
reach, its brief continuance, are the defects of the
spoken word, but when graven on the stone or
painted on the vellum it passes from one end of
the earth to the other for all time; it conquers at
once eternity and space.*

From the earliest ages the origin of language
has been a topic of discussion and speculation,
and a vast number of treatises have been written
upon it. But it is only in modern times that we
have collected sufficient data to admit of any
consistent or exhaustive theory, and the earlier †

* Charma, *Essai sur le Langage,* p. 60.
† "Ici comme ailleurs on a commencé par bâtir des systèmes,
au lieu de se borner à l'observation de faits."—Abel Rémusat.

writers contented themselves for the most part with building systems before they had collected facts.

There have been three main theories to account for the appearance of language, and it will be both interesting and instructive to pass them in brief review. They are :—1. That language was innate and organic. 2. That language was the result partly of imitation, and partly of convention. 3. That language was revealed. It will be seen from our consideration of them, that none of these theories is in itself wholly true or adequate, yet that each of them has a partial value, and that they are not so irreconcileably opposed to each other as might at first sight be imagined.

1. It was believed by the ancients generally, and perhaps by the majority of moderns, that language was *innate and organic; i.e.,* a distinct *creation* synchronising with the creation of man. The inferences drawn from this supposition led men to regard words as " types of objective reality, the shadow of the body and the image reflected in the mirror."* The words were sup-

---

* Bunsen, *Phil. of Un. Hist.* i. 40. The philosophers who held these views were called "Analogists," while those who leaned to the conventional origin of language were styled "Anomalista." But Plato and Aristotle admit the existence of both principles, and have written on the subject with a depth of philosophical insight,

posed to be not only a sign of the thing intended
by them, but in some way to partake of its nature,
and to express and symbolise something of its
idea. Hence the very notion of arbitrariness was
well-nigh expelled from language, and there was
supposed to be a deep harmony * between the
physiological quality of the sound and its significance—between the combination and connection
of sounds with the connection and combined
relations of the things they represented. Who-
ever, therefore, knew the names, knew also the
things which the names implied.† However

which, in spite of their defective knowledge, has never been surpassed. See Humboldt's *Cosmos*, i. 41, ii. 261.

* Plato's *Cratylus*, p. 423, et passim; and Schleiermacher's Introduction. The great authority on the ancient views of philology
is Lersch, *Sprachphilosophie der Alten*. (Bonn. 1838-1841.)
The question which agitated the schools was, φύσει τὰ ὀνόματα ἢ
θέσει; it was generally decided in favour of the "Analogists,"
though often for frivolous reasons. See Aul. Gell. *Noct. Att.* x.
4. (Renan, p. 137.) Cf. Xen. *Mem.* iv. 6. 1. Arrian, *Epict.*
i. 17, ii. 10. *Marc. Aur.* iii. 2; v. 8; x. 8. These views of the
mimetic character of words (Arist. *Rhet.* iii. 1, 2), and their
intrinsic connection with things, did not seem to be much disturbed
by the fact of the multiplicity of languages, although this fact led
Aristotle to place the conventional element first. The very word
βάρβαρος implies a lofty contempt for all languages except Greek,
and traces of a similar contempt may be found in the vocabulary
of many nations. Cf. Timtim, Zamzummim, &c., Renan, p. 178.
Pictet's *Origines Indo-Eur.* p. 56, seqq. (1 Cor. xiv. 11.)

† ὅς ἂν τὰ ὀνόματα [ἐπίστηται ἐπίστασθαι καὶ τὰ πράγματα.
Plato, *Crat.* 435, c. In proof that Plato *did* recognise both

strange and even ridiculous these views may appear to our somewhat superficial and unphilosophical age, it is far more difficult to understand them truly than to speak of them contemptuously, and they led to a reverence for the use of speech which reacted beneficially in producing careful writing and accurate thought.

The belief that language was innate led to the strange hallucination that if a child were entirely secluded from human contact, he would speak instinctively the primitive language of mankind. According to Herodotus, the experiment was actually made by Psammetichus, King of Egypt, who entrusted two new-born infants to a shepherd, with the injunction to let them suck a goat's milk, and to speak no words in their presence, but to observe what word they would first utter. After two years the shepherd visited them, and they approached him, stretching* out their hands, and uttering the word βεκός. It was found that this vocable existed in the Phrygian language, and meant " bread ; " whence it was sagely inferred that the Phrygians spoke the original language,

elements of language—the absolute and the conventional, see *Crat.* 435, c., and *Philol. Trans.* iii. 137. For an able exposition of the *Cratylus*, see Dr. Donaldson's *New Crat.* p. 93, seqq.

* Herodot. ii. 2.

and were the most ancient of people. There is
in this story such a delicious naïveté, that one
could hardly expect that it would have happened
in any except very early ages. It can, however,
be paralleled by the popular opinion which attributed the same experiment to James IV. and
Frederic II.* in the Middle Ages. In the latter
case the little unfortunates died for want of
lullabies ! Similarly, almost every nation has regarded its own language as the primitive one.
One of the historians of St. Louis says that a deaf
mute, miraculously healed at the king's tomb,
spoke, not in the language of Burgundy, where
he was born, but in the language† of the capital.
A similar belief seems to underlie the extreme
anxiety and curiosity of savages to learn the name
of any article hitherto unknown to them, as though

---

* Raumer, *Gesch. der Hohenstaufen*, iii. 491, quoted by Baehr,
Herod. l. c. For some other theories on the primitive language, see
Cardinal Wiseman's *Lectures on Science*, i. 19. Becanus supposed
seriously that Low Dutch was spoken in Paradise. *Hermathena*,
lib. ix. p. 204. "That children naturally speak Hebrew," is one
of the vulgar errors which had to be exploded even in the time of
Sir T. Browne. *Vulg. Err.* v. ch. 26. When James IV. of Scotland
repeated the experiment of Psammetichus, the infants were shut up
with a dumb man, and spoke Hebrew spontaneously ! Basque,
Swedish, Russ, &c., have all had their advocates. Charma, *Essai
sur le Langage*, p. 242, seqq. Leibnitz, *Lettre à M. de Sparren-
feld*, § 8.   † Renan, p. 147.

the name had some absolute significance. This is not the place to enter into a discussion of that deep germ of truth which such fancies involve; but hints of it may be found in Holy * Scripture.

No doubt at first sight it appears that much might be said in favour of the innate and organic nature of language. Its beauty,† its diversity, its power, its diffusion over the whole surface of the globe, give it the supernatural air of a gift which man, so far from originating, can only ruin and destroy. We see that in favourable situations language, like vegetation, flourishes and blossoms, while elsewhere it fades and dies away as a plant loses its foliage when deprived of nourishment and light. It seems, too, to participate in that healing power of nature, which effaces rapidly all trace of wounds received. Like nature, it produces mighty results out of feeble resources—it is economical without avarice, and liberal without prodigality.

Again; do we not see that almost every living thing is endowed in infinite variety with the

---

* There are some noble remarks to this effect in Schlegel's *Philosophische Vorlesungen*. Wiem. 1830. Hebrew scholars will readily remember cases of the importance attached by the sacred writers to the mere *sound* of words; a remarkable instance may be seen in Jer. i. 11, 12, and a curious play on sounds occurs in the second verse of Genesis.   † Grimm, s. 12.

faculty of uttering sounds, and even of inter-communicating feelings? *   The air is thrilled with the voice of birds, and some of them even possess a power of articulation, which among many nations is the distinctive † definition of man. Nay, fancy has attributed to animals a power of language in the age of gold—a power which under certain ‡ circumstances they are supposed to be still allowed to exercise.

But this leads us to the true point of difference. The dog barks, as it barked § at the creation, and the crow of the cock is the same now as when it reached the ear of repentant Peter. The song of the nightingale, and the howl of the leopard, have continued as unchangeable as the concentric

---

* "I am by no means clear that the dog may not have an analogon of words."—Coleridge. Similarly Plato attributes a διάλεκτος to animals, adducing some very interesting proofs. See Clemens Alexandr. *Strom.* i. 21, § 413. See, too, Thomsou's *Passions of Animals.* "They also know, and reason not contemptibly."—Milton.

† μέροπες βροτοί.—Homer, passim.

‡ As in the instance of Balaam.—Numb. 22.   Cf. Tibull. ii. v. 78. Hom. *Il.* τ. 407, &c.

§ Dr. Latham points out that this statement requires modification ; e.g., it is doubtful whether a *howl*, and not a bark, is not the organic and instinctive sound uttered by dogs. (*Encycl. Brit.* Art. *Language.*) Still we do not anticipate that any one will dispute the general proposition. See Heyse, *System der Sprachwissenschaft,* § 25.

circles of the spider, and the waxen hexagon of the bee. The one as much as the other are the result of a blind though often perfect instinct. They are unalterable because they are innate, and the utterances of mankind would have been as unchangeable as those of animals, had they been in the same way the result not of liberty but of necessity. To the cries of animals we must compare, not man's ever-varying language, but those instinctive sounds of weeping, sobbing, moaning—the changeless scream, sigh, or laughter —by which, since the creation, he has given relief or expression to his physical * sensations.

In point of fact—as a thousand experiments might have proved to Psammetichus—a new-born infant possesses the faculty of language, not actually, but only potentially. It is obvious that an Italian infant, picked up on the field of Solferino and carried to Paris, would not have spoken Italian but French, and an English babe, carried off by the Caffirs, would find no difficulty in learning the rich language of Caffraria, with its five-and-twenty moods. For language is clearly learned by *imitation*. This is the intermediate

* Grimm, 13, 14. "Language," he adds (p. 17), "can only be compared to the cries of animals, in respect that both are subjected to certain physical conditions of organism."

link between the δύναμις and the ἔργον. When
poor Kaspar Hauser tottered into the streets of
Nüremburg, the only words he could say were,
"I will be a soldier as my father was," because
those were the only words which he had heard
in his miserable confinement. Doubtless, the
Egyptian children pronounced the word βεκός,
because it approached as nearly as possible to
the bleating * of the goat by which they had been
suckled.

Had there ever been an innate organic language, it is quite certain that it must have left
some traces ; for, as Dr. Latham observes, "language (as an instrument of criticism in ethnology)
is *the most permanent* of the criteria of human

---

* "On a très judicieusement remarqué sur celle-ci," says M.
Nodier, "que la seule induction qui en résultât naturellement,
fort concluante pour la langue primitive et immodifiable des
chèvres ne prouvoit rien en faveur de la première langue de
l'homme ; puisque les chèvres formoient elles-mêmes d'une manière
très-distincte les deux articulations dont ces enfants avoient com-
posé leur étroit vocabulaire." Sir Gardner Wilkinson discredits
the whole story, and supposes that it originated among the Greek
ciceroni in Egypt, because he thinks that children, unless artificially instructed, would not have been able to get beyond the
labial sound "be." (Rawlinson's *Herodotus*, i. 251.) Surely this
is merely a begging of the question. The fact that the inference
from the experiment was one unfavourable to the national vanity
of the Egyptians, is only one of the reasons which induce us to
credit its reality. Larcher (ad loc.) rightly regards the os as merely
the Greek termination.

relationships derivable from our moral constitution." Talleyrand's wicked witticism, that " language was given us to conceal our thoughts," arose from the fact that it is used for that purpose on a thousand occasions. But although a man may "coin his face into smiles," and utter a thousand honeyed words, his real sentiments *will* flash out sometimes in passionate gesture and rapid glance ; and just in the same way, had there even been a language which was the organic expression of emotion, it is absolutely impossible that it should have wholly disappeared. That which is really implanted is for the most part unalterable.

2. Seeing, then, that positive experiment, as well as other considerations, disprove the inneity of language, other philosophers believed that it was simply conventional, and grew up gradually after a period of mutism. The Epicurean philosophy, deeply tainted with the error of man's slow and toilsome development from a savage and almost bestial * condition, gave the problem the

* "Mutum et turpe pecus."—Hor. *Sat.* i. 3. 99. Similar views are to be found in Diod. Sic. i. 1 ; Vitruv. *Archit.* ii. 1. " Thrown as it were by chance on a confused and savage land, an orphan abandoned by the unknown hand that had produced him." —Volney. Epicurus thought that men spoke just as dogs bark, φυσικῶς κινούμενοι.

hardest of all material solutions. This school
found in Lucretius its most splendid exponent,
and the poet accounts for the appearance of
speech as the gradual and instinctive endeavour
to supply a want.* In short, words came because
they were required, much in the same way that,
according to the theory of Lamarck, organic
peculiarities are the result of habit and instinct,
so that the crane acquired a long neck and long
legs by persevering attempts to fish. Lucretius
compares language to the widely diverse sounds
which animals emit to express different sensations,
and, scornfully rejecting the theory of one Name-
giver, asserts repeatedly that—

"Utilitas* expressit nomina rerum."

It was generally believed by this school that
man originally acquired the faculty of speech by
an observation of the sounds of nature. The
cries of animals, " the hollow murmuring wind
and silver rain," the sighing of the woods,

* Lucret. v. 1027—1089. The whole passage is one of remarkable beauty and ingenuity. Neither Epicurus nor Lucretius ex-
cluded altogether the innate element; v. Diog. Laert. x. 75, sq.
Lucretius rightly regards language as no less natural than
gesticulation, and so might have taught a lesson to Reid and
Dugald Stewart. See Fleming's *Vocab. of Philosophy*, s. v. *Language*. The whole theory is stated and ridiculed by Lactantius,
Instit. Div. vi. 10.

"The tongue of forests green and flowery wilds,"

these, it seems, were man's * teachers in the power of articulation.

> " The joyous birds shrouded in cheerful shade,
>   Their notes unto the voice attempted sweet ;
> Th' angelical soft trembling voices made
>   To th' instruments divine respondence meet,
> With the base murmurs of the water's fall ;
>   The water's fall with difference discreet,
> Now soft, now loud, unto the wind did call ;
> The gentle warbling wind low answerèd to all." †

Man, too, would endeavour to take his part in the divine harmony ; he would translate into living and intelligent utterances the dim and sublime music of this unconscious hymn.

Like most theories that have met with any amount of acceptance, this belief contains a germ

* He began
> " In murmurs which his first endeavoring tongue
> Caught infant-like from the far-foamèd sands."

An extremely curious Esthonian legend (the only one which Grimm has discovered bearing any resemblance to the Babel-dispersion) seems to involve the same conception. God, seeing that population was too crowded, determined to disperse man, by giving to each nation a distinct tongue. Accordingly, he placed on the fire a caldron full of water, and made the different races successively approach, who appropriated respectively the various sounds of the hissing and singing water.—Grimm, p. 28. Others have compared with it the Mexican legend about the doves. See Winer, *Biblisches Realwörterb.* s. v. *Sprache.*

† Spenser's *Faërie Queen.*

of truth. It originated from the on'omatopœic
character of a large part of all languages.
But we reject the conclusion drawn from this
fact. That man produced a large or very large
part of his vocabulary by an imitation of natural
sounds is entirely true, but that the idea of
speech was created in him by the hearing of
those sounds we believe to be eminently false.
This theory, however, found especial favour
among the philosophers of the eighteenth century, except that with them a mysterious convention seemed not even to require this natural
basis. Maupertuis, Condillac, Rousseau, Volney,
Nodier, Herder, Monboddo, and Dr. Smith,* all
seem to believe in an original time when a few
intonations, joined to gesture and expression of
the face, sufficed for the wants of nascent
humanity, and formed, in fact, a natural language ;
but in course of time this was found inadequate,
and so " on convint,† on s'arrangea à l'aimable,
et ainsi fut établi le *langage artificiel* ou articulé."
According to Monboddo the steps of the process

---

* For assertions of the conventional character of language, see
Arist. περὶ Ἑρμηνείας, ii. 1. Plato, *Crat.* ad in. Harris, *Hermes*,
iii. 1. Locke, iii. 1—8. Fénélon, *Lettre sur les occupations de
l'Acad.* § 3. (These are quoted at length by Charma, p. 208.)
Smith, *Theory of the Moral Sentiments*, ii. 364. Grimm, 39, 40.
Lersch, *passim*.   † Renan, p. 78.

were briefly as follows:—1, Inarticulate cries;
2, Gestures; 3, Imitative sounds; 4, An artificial
language, formed by convention, and resulting
from the necessities of the race. This language
was originally poor and defective, but developed
into richness, just as (to quote the simile of Adelung) the canoe of the savage has grown into the
floating city of modern nations. All other conjectures are, however, eclipsed by Dr. Murray's
derivation of all the languages of Europe from
nine onomatopœic syllables. These wondrous
vocables * were :—1, Ag ; 2, Bag ; 3, Dwag ;
4, Cwag; 5, Lag; 6, Mag; 7, Nag; 8, Rag;
9, Swag!!! M. Renan (who believes that *all* the
parts of speech existed implicitly in the primitive
language) may well remark that of all theories
this is "the most false, or rather the least rich in
truth;" and it may be known by its fruits, for the
natural inference from it is either " that † thought

* See Wiseman, p. 54. This theory of the development of
human language required the supposition of an indefinite period
of human existence; but even if this be freely admitted, it is
impossible to prove the *first step* by which unarticulated sounds,
the *merely passive* echoes of blind instincts or outward phenomena,
could develop into the expression of thought. See Bunsen, ii. 76.
It would have been marvellous indeed, if man had by the mere
possession of vocal cries, not differing from those of animals, been
able to raise himself from the utterances of instinct and appetite to
express the emotions of admiration, hope, and love. See Nodier,
Notions, p. 14.   † Bunsen, ii. 130.
c 2

is merely an affection of perishable matter (*ma-terialism*), or that both are indiscriminately acci-dents of the one divine substance of the universe (*pantheism*)." It is true that language, though not the result of convention, tends to *become* * conventional in the process of time, but this very tendency is often a mark of decay and ruin, and a language is a noble and powerful instrument of thought in proportion as it keeps in view the motives and principles which originated the words of which it is composed.

3. The third main theory, which has found numberless supporters, is, that *language is due to direct revelation.* The tenacity of this belief was mainly due to the violent reaction of the spiri-tualist school in the nineteenth century against the systematising scepticism of their predecessors. It was warmly adopted by MM. de Bonald, de Maistre, De Lammenais, and others, and was in one sense a step forwards, for it recognised at least that "divine† spark which glows in all

---

* Thus words and phrases repeatedly acquire a conventional meaning for a generation, and then recur to their old sense. Almost every sect, every profession, and even every family, have certain words in use to which they attach a peculiar and special meaning, which is sometimes unintelligible to others. M. Cousin has been unable to discover the meaning which the Port-Royalists attached to the word "machine." See Charma, p. 209.

† Wilhelm von Humboldt, *Lettre à M. Abel Rémusat.* Paris, 1827.

idioms even the most imperfect and uncultivated."
But this theory must likewise be rejected. It
raises * men to the level of gods, as much as the
former theory had degraded them to the rank of
beasts. " Spiritualism contradicts nature, as
materialism contradicts mind. It has reality and
history against it as much as its opposite."

This view opens considerations of such importance that we must subject it to a still more
careful discussion.

We object, in the first place, to the difficulty
and obscurity of the phrase. In ' one sense,†
indeed—if we take it metaphorically,—it is
perhaps the most exact expression to describe
the wonderful apparition of human speech, which
it rightly withdraws from the sphere of vulgar
inventions. Language, as an immediate product of

---

* Grimm, § 28.

† In the following observations, I quote the thoughts of M.
Renan, pp. 81—83. I have not used inverted commas, because I
have often transposed and abbreviated his actual words. Very
similar are the excellent remarks of Nodier, which are too apposite
to be omitted. "On ne me soupçonnera pas d'être d'assez
mauvais goût pour avoir attendu à substituer mes théories aux
faits de révélation... Je crois fermement que la parole a été donnée
à l'homme, comme je le crois de toutes les facultés que la création a
réparti entre les créatures. Le seul point sur lequel j'ose différer
des casuistes du son littéral, c'est que ce don ne me paroît pas
avoir consisté dans la communication d'un système lexicologique
tout fait, &c."—*Notions de Linguistique*, p. 9.

human powers, might perhaps, with more safety,
be attributed to the Universal Cause, than to the
particular action of human liberty. If by revelation be intended *the spontaneous play of the
human faculties*, in this sense, God, having endowed man with all things requisite for the discovery of language, may, with near approximation
to truth, be called its Author; but then, why
make use of an expression so indirect and liable
to be misunderstood, when others more natural
and more philosophical might have been found
to indicate the same* fact?

But, unhappily, M. de Bonald and others who
urged this view took the expression literally, and
made it not scientific but theological; not a dis-
interested † and independent conclusion drawn

* A beautiful illustration of Herder's will help to show our
meaning. "Observe," he says, "this tree with its vigorous
trunk, its magnificent crown of verdure, its branches, its foliage,
its flowers, its fruits, raising itself upon its roots as on a throne.
Seized with admiration and astonishment, you exclaim, 'It is divine,
divine !' Now observe this little seed ; see it hidden in the earth,
then pushing out a feeble germ, covering itself with buds, clothing
itself with leaves ; you will again exclaim, 'It is divine !' but in
a manner more worthy and more intelligent."

† Nothing has been more fatally prejudicial to the progress of
science than a theological bias in its votaries ; and nothing more
fatal to the peace of true discoverers than its ignorant tyranny.
Adelung shows true wisdom in prefacing his *Mithridates* with the
statement, "Ich habe keine Lieblingsmeinung, keine Hypothese

from induction, but a mere dogma of faith to be forced (like so many other false excrescences of theological tradition) upon the conscience of all Christians. In general, those who maintain the literal revelation of language, and reject its human origin, are the direct successors of those theologians who have so long opposed every discovery in science, and rejected the plainest deductions of geometry and logic. They intrude into a sphere in which they have no knowledge and no place; their arguments are neither scientific nor reasonable; they are not reasons but assertions; not conclusions but idle and groundless prejudices. It has been well said that they pertain to an order of ideas and interests which science repudiates, and with which she has nothing to do. Ignorance has no claim to a hearing even when she speaks *ex cathedrâ*.

Now what is meant by such an expression as the revelation of language rigorously understood? If, for instance, we take it materially, if we understand it to mean that a voice from heaven dictated to men the names of things—such a conception is so grossly * anthropomorphic, it is

zum Grunde zu legen. Noah's Arche ist mir eine Verschlossene Burg, und Babylon's Schutt bleibt vor mir völlig in seiner Ruhe."

* It seems to me, however, that Grimm's special arguments on this subject are weak (p. 26); he is clearly right in pointing out

so utterly at variance with all scientific explanation, it is so irreconcileably opposed to all our
ideas of the laws of nature, that it needs no
refutation for one who is in the least degree
initiated into the methods of modern criticism.
Besides, as M. Cousin* has remarked, "it only
removes the difficulty a step backwards without
resolving it. For signs divinely invented would
for us not be *signs* but *things*, which we should
have been subsequently obliged to elevate into
signs by attaching to them certain significations."
The revealed "term" would be a useless encum-
brance unless it corresponded with some well
understood conception; and therefore if words
were revealed, conceptions must also have been
implanted; and we are thus driven to the
absurdity of supposing that anterior to all experience, we knew that which experience (*i. e.* an†
actual relation of intelligence with that which is
the object of intelligence) alone could teach us.

We have already said that these modern
spiritualists considered the revelation of language to be a truth involved by the narrative of

the futility of such conjectures as those of Lessing, that language
was made known to man by intercourse with intermediate spirits.
(Lessing, *Simmtl. Schriften*, Bd. 10.)

* *Préface aux Œuvres Philos. de Maine de Biran*, iv. p. xv.
† Charma, *Essai sur le Langage*, p. 129.

Genesis. In this they were the slaves of a false and narrow exegesis, which had not even the poor excuse of being literal. What is the true meaning of the sacred writer we shall endeavour to show further on; but we cannot here abstain from again uttering a strong protest against the barrier placed in the way of all honest scientific inquiry by the timid prejudices of that class which tyrannises over public opinion. When shall we learn to acquiesce practically in the belief which theoretically the most orthodox have long expressed, that it is a needless incongruity to look in the Bible for scientific truths which it does not profess to reveal? "Such * an attempt," it has been well said, "has been *a perversion of the purpose of a divine revelation, and cannot lead to any physical truth.*"

Honesty all the more imperiously demands this remark, because here, as in a thousand other places, perverted by system and ignorance, we believe that the Bible rightly understood contains (not precise dogmas, but) the general indications of a sublime truth; and because it may be shown

* Dr. Whewell, *Hist. of Ind. Science*, iii. 504. A host of eminent authorities, from Bacon down to Sir John Herschel, have said the same thing;—hitherto, alas, in vain ! See Herschel's *Letter to Dr. Pye Smith.* Mill's *Dissert.* i. 435—461. Renan, *Hist. Rel.* xxvii. Charma, p. 248.

that in this particular instance *its records accu·
rately agree with the results of careful and
laborious inquiry.*   Here, as often, the Bible
does not clash with the conclusions of science,
if taken *to imply no more than what it categori-
cally asserts.*   But the Bible is not the *only*
source of information open to us, and if we are
ever in any way to fill up "the vast lacunas
which characterise that gigantic and mysterious
epitaph of humanity engraved in the first chapters of Genesis," we must do so not by ignorant
and dogmatic assertions, but by humble sincerity
and patient research.

If, then, language were revealed, the Bible is
not only silent on such a revelation, but distinctly implies the reverse. We shall examine
the narrative of Genesis (ii. 19, 20) farther on;
but we must here stop to observe that where the
Deity is represented as talking to Adam and
other patriarchs, such passages must not be supposed to have any bearing on the question, as it
is quite clear that they are only intended for an
expressive anthropomorphism.*   Even Luther,

---

* St. Gregory of Nyssa has expressed himself on this subject
with startling freedom of thought. He alludes with ironic pity
to those who speak of the Deity as the fabricator of Adam's
language, an opinion which he expressly calls a sottish and
ridiculous vanity, quite worthy of the extravagant presumption

in his Commentary on Genesis, goes out of his
way to prove that nothing material is intended
in such phrases as God's " speaking to " Adam,
and that it would be as strange to suppose that
they imply any* revelation of language, as it
would be to infer the revelation of writing from
the mention of the stone tables " written by the
finger of God." Writing also has been attributed
directly to God's external gift, although, as in
the case of language, there is the clearest proof
of its human origin and gradual perfectionment.

But we must not omit one or two positive
arguments against this theory.

1. Had language been revealed, mankind at
first would have been better situated than any of
their posterity; and such a disposition is unlike
the ordinary course of God's just dealings.

of the Jews. And on the subject of Babel, he says, "The confusion of tongues must be necessarily attributed to the will of
God according to the theologic point of view, but according to the
truth of history it is the work of man."—*Contra Eunomium,*
Or. xii. p. 782. Nodier, p. 56. St. Augustin distinctly implies
the same thing.—*De Ord.* ii. 12.

* Since writing the above, I have met with another Biblical
argument in favour of the Revelation of Language, drawn from
Gen. i. 5. καὶ τὸ μὲν φῶς ἐκάλεσεν ὁ Θεὸς ἡμέραν, τὸ δὲ σκότος
νύκτα· ἐπεί τοι γε ἄνθρωπος οὐκ ἂν ᾔδει καλεῖν τὸ φῶς ἡμέραν ἢ
τὸ σκότος νύκτα. ἀλλ' οὐδὲ μὲν τὰ λοιπὰ, εἰ μὴ τὴν ὀνομασίαν
εἰλήφει ἀπὸ τοῦ ποιήσαντος αὐτὰ Θεοῦ.—Theophil. *ad Autolyc.* ii.

2. So far from being "a pale image and feeble echo of splendours which have passed away from the scene of earth," each human language bears in itself the most distinct traces of growth and progress—the marks of a regular development in accordance with definite laws—the successive traces of infancy, youth, maturity, and manhood. Though many existing languages, and even those of some savage nations are but "degraded and decaying fragments of nobler formations," yet there are proofs as decisive that they rose to gradual perfection, as that they subsequently fell from perfection to decay.   ♥

3. If the spiritualist theory were true, it would be a most natural inference that the spiritual and abstract signification of roots is also the original one. But such an assumption (although it is made by Frederic Schlegel), "is contra-dicted by the history of every language of the world."

4. It is equally improbable that God who revealed the primitive language, or man who received it, should have suffered it (divine, as on this supposition it must have been) to degenerate into barbarous and feeble jargons.

18. ed. Wolf p. 140.   I present this argument without reply to any one who is convinced by it.

5. "The human faculties *are competent* to the formation of *language." It is therefore totally unlike God's methods, as observed in His works, to give *directly* what can be evolved *mediately*. For there is clearly no waste in the economy of Nature, no prodigality in the display of miracles. In the words of Grimm, "it seems contrary to the wisdom of God to impose the restraint of a created form on that which was destined to a free historic development." At any rate, as a fact we *can* historically trace the development of language from a very small nucleus, and this being the case the supposition of any previous revealed language is a groundless and improbable hypothesis.†

Further arguments will appear as we proceed; but we must now point out the true meaning of the statement in Genesis, that "God brought all living creatures to Adam *to see what he would call them;* and whatsoever Adam called every

---

* Stewart, *Phil. of the Mind*, iii. 1.

† "This method of referring words immediately to God as their framer, is a short cut to escape inquiry and explanation. It saves the philosopher much trouble, but leaves mankind in great ignorance, and leads to great error. *Non dignus vindice nodus.* God having furnished man with senses, and with organs of articulation, as he has also with water, lime, and sand, it should seem no more necessary to form the words for man, than to temper the mortar."—*Divers. of Purley*, Pt. i. ch. 2.

living creature that was the name thereof."[*]
Now, merely remarking (by way of limitation)
that the writer clearly supposed his own language
to be that of Paradise, and that there is here no
attempt to account for all[†] language, because he
is speaking of a certain class of words only—we
find in this narrative a profound verity clothed in
a most beautiful and appropriate symbol: 'We
see man as the true nomenclator—man acting by
his own peculiar faculties under the guide of the
Deity.   Philosophy[‡] could find no more perfect
figure to express her conclusions than this—God
teaching man to speak as a father would a son.'
But to give this simple narrative a material
explanation is to falsify at once both its letter
and its spirit.   On the other hand, "to say with
the theologians that God had created language[§]

* Gen. ii. 19, 20.

† e. g. There is no hint of *grammar*, the very blood of language.
"Une Langue n'est pas une seule collection des mots."—Cousin,
Cours de 1829, iii. 212.

‡ Renan, p. 85. See an eloquent passage of Schlegel's to the
same effect, quoted in Wiseman's *Lect.* i. 108. Pythagoras probably had some vague sentiment of the kind when he said that
"the namegiver" was both the most ancient and the most rational
of men. The Egyptians worshipped Theuth as the Regulator of
Language ; and the Chinese referred its origin to their great mysterious King Fohi. See Cic. *Tusc. Disp.* i. 28. Lersch, *die
Sprachphilos. der Alten.* Bonn, 1838, i. 23—29.

§ Bunsen, i. 49.

as he had created man, and that language is not
the act and work of man," is to contradict not
only reason but the Bible too. For be it observed, that the Bible distinctly confirms our
arguments by saying, not that *God* named the
animals, but that *Adam* named them, and that
whatsoever *he* named every living creature *that*
was the name thereof.

In short, language is "only divine in proportion to the divinity of our nature and our soul;"
it is only a gift of God because the faculty
naturally resulted from the physical and spiritual
organism which God had created. This seems a
more natural and philosophic supposition than
the belief that even the *embryonic germ* of language was revealed. The exercise of the faculty
in the original utterance of primitive words has
ceased to be called into play because it has
ceased to be required. We cannot now invent
original words because there is no longer any
necessity for doing so. In the same way—as is
well known—a deaf mute when once instructed
in an artificial language loses the quick instinctive power of creating intelligible natural signs.

We conclude, then, that language is neither
innate and organic; nor a mechanical invention;
nor an external gift of revelation;—but a natural

faculty swiftly developed by a powerful instinct, the result of intelligence * and human freedom which have no place in purely organic † functions. It was "the living product of the whole ‡ inner man." It was "not§ a gift bestowed ready formed to man, but something coming from himself." It is "essentially ‖ human; it owes to our full liberty both its origin and its progress; it is our history, our heritage." Objectively considered, it was the result of organism: subjectively, the product of intelligence. It was "a primitive intuition, impersonal and yet influenced by individual genius;" in a word, its character is "at once ¶ objective and subjective, at once individual and general, at once free and necessary, at once·human and divine."

That such a conclusion,** however much it may

---

* The fact that man is a social animal (ζῷον πολιτικὸν) which has been so strangely urged by the advocates of a revealed language, from Lactantius down to M. de Bonald and the Abbé Combalot, in no way militates against this conclusion.

† Heyse, *System der Sprachwissenschaft*, § 50.

‡ Schlegel.

§ Wil. von Humboldt.

‖ Grimm.

¶ Renan.

** The Revelation of Language is supported in a book by J. S. Süssmilch, Berlin, 1766. An excellent review of the main opinions is given by R. W. Zobel, *Gedanken über die verschiedenen*

seem to savour of a weak eclecticism by combining all former theories, is yet in profound accordance with all the ascertained facts of language we shall hope to prove in the following chapter.

Meinungen der Gelehrnten von Ursprunge der Sprachen. Magdeb. 1733.

CHAPTER II.

THE PSYCHOLOGICAL DEVELOPMENT OF THE IDEA OF SPEECH.

> " Speech is morning to the mind ;
> It spreads the beauteous images abroad,
> Which else lie dark and buried in the soul."

FROM abstract and *à priori* considerations, we have arrived at the conclusion that language was achieved or created by the human race, by the unconscious or spontaneous exercise of divinely implanted powers; that it was a faculty analogous to and closely implicated with that of thought, and, like thought, developing itself with * the aid of time. The idea of speech was innate, and the evolution of that idea may be traced in the growth and history of language. It is most important to have a clear conception of the fact that this development did not result

---

* See Franck's *Dictionnaire des Sciences Philosophiques*, Art. *Signes.* I must here again caution the reader that the view here supported is *not* the conventional theory of language condemned in the last chapter, although it might easily become so in the hands of a person inclined to look at the physiological rather than the psychological aspects of the question.

from an atomistic* reunion of parts, but from
the vitality derived from an inward principle.
Language was formed by a process not of crystal-
line accretion but of germinal development.
Every essential part of language existed as completely (although only implicitly) in the primitive
germ, as the petals of a flower exist in the bud
before the mingled influences of the sun and the
air have caused it to unfold.

Our belief thus arrived at—viz., that language
was an achievement of the human genius which
God implanted in the primeval man, a development of the faculty with which he endowed our
race—does not at all necessitate the belief in a
period when man was unable to communicate
with man. The exercise of the faculty may have
been rapid in that young and noble nature to a
degree which now we cannot even conceive. A
few imitative roots, uttered under the guidance
of a divine instinct, and aided by the play of
intelligence in movement and feature, would with
wonderful ease grow into a language sufficient
for the needs of a nascent humanity, and the
living germ would soon bud and bourgeon by
the very law of its production. Even if we were

* This is an expression of F. Schlegel's (*Philos. Vorlesungen*, p.
78—80). Renan also quotes the authority of Humboldt and Goethe.

compelled to believe that this language was at
first of the scantiest character, we see in this
supposition nothing more absurd than in the
certainty that knowledge and science, philosophy
and art, are the slow, gradual, and toilsome conquests of an ever progressive race. It is now
well understood that even the use of the senses
has to be learnt,—that it is only by practice that
we are able to discriminate distances in the
variously-coloured surface which is all that we
really see. Why should it then be unnatural to
suppose that speech also was at first only implicitly bestowed on us, and that it required time
and experience to develop fully the implanted
capacity ?

How far the growth of language was affected
by external circumstances,—as, for instance, by
the impress of individual minds, by the aristo-
cracy or even autocracy of philosophic bodies, by
the influence of sex, by the variations of climate,
by the convulsions of history, by the slow change
of religious or political convictions, and even by
the laws of euphony and organisation, we may
consider hereafter ; but we must first of all enter
on two very interesting preliminary inquiries, viz.,
1, How did words first come to be accepted as
signs at all ? and, 2, By what processes did men

hit upon the words themselves ?   Or, to put the
questions differently : 1, How did various modulations of the human voice acquire any significance by being connected with outward or inward
phenomena ? and, 2, What special causes led in
special cases to the choice of some particular
modulations rather than of any other ?

I am well aware that these questions may
appear ridiculous to any one who is entirely
unaccustomed to these branches of inquiry ; and
they may possibly be inclined to set the whole
matter at rest by a dogmatism or a jeer.   They
will say perhaps :

> " Here babbling Insight shouts in Nature's ears
> His last conundrum of the orbs and spheres ;
> There Self-inspection sucks his little thumb,
> With 'Whence am I ?' and 'Wherefore did I come ?' " *

With readers of such a temperament it is idle to
reason, nor do we expect that, while the world
lasts, ignorance will cease to take itself for knowledge, and denounce what it cannot understand.
To others we will merely say that these inquiries
have occupied, and are still occupying in an

---

* "Seht, es ist schwer zu denken auf welche Art man denkt.
. . . Ich denke, und mit dem Zeuge, womit Ich denke, soll ich
denken wie dieses Zeug beschaffen sei," &c.—Tieck, *Blaubart*,
act. ii. sc. 1.

increasing degree, some of the most profound and
sober intellects in Europe, and that (in the words
of Plato) 'wise men do not usually talk non-
sense.'

With this remark, let us proceed to our first
question : How came sounds—mere vibrations of
the atmosphere—to be accepted as signs, *i. e.* to
be used as words ?

But (as one inquiry leads us back, perpetually,
to another, even until " all things end in a
mystery "), we must here again pause for a
moment to ask what *is* a word ? So vast an
amount has been written in answer to this
inquiry, that it is obviously impossible to do
more than state the conclusion* we adopt, with a
mere hint as to the ground on which we adopt it.

Horne Tooke maintained that words are " the
names of things," a definition most obviously inadequate ; others have called them " the pictures
of ideas,"† and although this definition is not
without its value, yet the systematic perversion of
the word " idea," renders it insufficient. Harris

---

* We are, for instance, obliged entirely to pass over the question
as to the Primum Cognitum, on which see Sir W. Hamilton's
Lectures, ii. 319—331.

† " One might be tempted to call Language a kind of Picture of
the Universe, where the words are as the figures and images of all
particulars."—Harris's *Hermes,* p. 330. This is something like

devotes a chapter to establishing the definition
that "Words are the symbols of ideas, both
general and particular; yet, of the general,
primarily, essentially, and immediately; of the
particular only secondly, accidentally, and mediately." But this is very questionable and
cumbrous; and, on the whole, we believe that no
better definition can be given than that of the
late Mr. Garnett,* that words represent " *conceptions* founded on *perceptions*," or "that words
express the *relations* of things." They do not
and cannot express " an intrinsic meaning, con-
stituting them the counterparts and equivalents
of thought. They *are* nothing more, and *can* be
nothing more, than signs of relations, and it is a
contradiction in terms to affirm that a relation
can be inherent." " Our knowledge of beings,"
says M. Peisse,† " is purely indirect, limited, relative; it does not reach to the beings themselves
in their absolute reality and essences, but only to
their accidents, their modes, their relations, their
limitations, their differences, their qualities; all

Plato's curious notion that words are a μίμησις of external things.
—Heyse, *System*, s. 24. ἐοικέναι γὰρ τὰ ὀνόματα .... 'εικόσι τῶν
ὁρατῶν.—Heraclitus, *ap. Ammonium ad Arist. de Interp.* p. 24.
Democritus called them ἀγάλματα φωνήεντα.

* Garnett's *Essays*, p. 281—341.
† Quoted by Mr. Garnett, p. 283.

which are manners of conceiving and knowing,
which not only do not impart to knowledge the
absolute character which some persons attribute
to it, but even positively exclude it. Matter (or
existence, the object of sensible perception), only
falls within the sphere of our knowledge through
its qualities; mind only by its modifications;
and these qualities and modifications are all that
can be comprehended and expressed in the object.
The object itself, considered absolutely, remains
out of the reach of all perception.'' It is an
obvious inference that, as we can only talk of
what we know, and as we can only know the relations of things, words *are the medium of expressing* (not the *nature* of things, which is incog-
nisable), but the *observed relations between things.*
They are revelations not of the outward, but of the
inward,—not of the universe, but of the thoughts
of man.

Leaving to metaphysicians all further discussion of this question, we again recur to our
inquiry, How came words to be accepted as significant of these relations ?   Thought* and speech

* Grimm, 29—31. Compare Heyse, *System*, s. 28. "Nur
was gedacht ist, kann gesprochen werden ; und das klar gedachte
ist nothwendig auch ansprechbar." What St. Paul saw in his
rapture was only unutterable because it recalled no human
analogon. (2 Cor. xii. 4.)

are inseparably connected; the very root of the word Man* implies, in Sanskrit, "a thinking being," and it is well known that there is a close connection between "ratio" and "oratio," and that ἄλογα ζῶα means animals, not only "without speech," but "without reason." Eloquence, in fact, is genius, and the greatest poet or orator is he who has most command over his native tongue.

It has even been a question with some philosophers whether thought is *possible* without speech,—whether, for instance, blind-deaf-mutes (like the American girl, Laura Bridgman), are capable† of exercising the faculty of reason until they have been taught an artificial method of expression ?

---

* Manudscha, Goth. Manniska, Germ. Mensch; from the root man, "to think." Compare φράζειν, "to speak," and φράζεσθαι, "to think."—Heyse, s. 40. Turner ad Herod. ii. 7.

† "Speech, "says Humboldt, "is the necessary condition of the thought of the individual." The statement should at least be qualified by the word "now." For some allusions to this interesting discussion, see Archbishop Whately's *Logic*, ch. ii. M. de Bonald *assumed* the reverse : "L'homme pense sa parole *avant* de parler sa pensée." See, too, Mill's *Logic*, ii. 201. Charma, p. 134. Of course the short-hand of human intelligence is too infinitely rapid and abbreviated for us to be always able to read it off with facility ; or, as Mr. Tennyson expresses it,

"Thought leapt out to wed with thought,
    Ere thought could wed itself to speech ;"

but we are inclined to believe that without *some* signs (not necessarily words—see Charma, *Essai sur le Langage*, p. 50)

Certain it is that the child begins to *speak* when it begins to *think*, and that its first intelligent perception of relations is followed by its first articulate utterances. We may illustrate this remark in an interesting manner. We find it stated in the Jadschurveda, that the first words uttered by the first man were, "I am myself," and that, when called, he answered, "I am he." With all due deference to the ancient philosopher who held this belief, we may safely assert that such a thing was impossible without some special interposition ; for the growth of a sense of individuality is extremely slow, and comes to children long after their main perceptions. A poet —in whom nothing is more remarkable than his profound learning and metaphysical accuracy— truly says : ·

> " The baby new to earth and sky,
>   What time his tender palm is prest
>   Against the circle of the breast,
>   Hath never thought that ' This is I :'

---

thought could not exist. When we cannot express what we mean, the reason probably is that we have no *clear* meaning. "Die Sprache ist nichts anderes als der in die Erscheinung tretende Gedanke, und beide sind innerlich *nur eins und das selbe*."—Becker, *Organism. der Sprache*, p. 2. "Sans signes nous ne penserions presque pas."—Destutt de Tracy, *Idéologie*, pt. xvii. Plotinus distinctly asserts the contrary. Τὸ δὴ λογιζόμενον τῆς ψυχῆς οὐδένος πρὸς τὸ λογίζεσθαι δεόμενον σωματικοῦ ὀργάνου.—*Ennead*, v. 1, ch. 10

But as he grows he gathers much,
    And learns the use of 'I' and 'me,'
    And finds 'I am not what I see,
    And other than the things I touch.' " *

And this gives us at once the true explanation
of the fact, that it is some time before a child
learns to regard itself as a subject, and therefore,
that it† objectises itself in all its language.   It
would say, not " I want an apple," but " Charlie
wants an apple ; " not even " give *me*,"—so frequently as "give Charlie."   When Hamlet signs
himself as ' The machine that is to me Hamlet,'
he only shows, by an extreme instance, the
remarkable difficulty that a man always has in
mastering this very conception of individuality,
which the Hindoo philosophy would seem to
regard as a primitive intuition.

By these remarks we have greatly cleared the
way for our explanation of the manner in which
words originated ; — an explanation‡ which is

---

* *In Memoriam.*
† See Harper, *on the Force of the Greek Tenses.*
‡ *Der Ursprung der Sprache.* Berlin, 1851. We closely follow
M. Renan's exposition as given in his preface, pp. 31, sq. Heyse
sums it up in one sentence, "Man kann mithin in dem Worte
ein dreifaches Moment unterscheiden : 1. die Lautform ; 2. das
dadurch bezeichnete in Sprachbewusstsein liegende Merkmal der
Vorstellung ; 3. den reinen Begriff, welchen der denkende Geist
in seiner Erhebung über die Individuelle Vorstellungsweise bildet,

purely psychological, and which was first promulgated in this shape by M. Steinthal.

Man has the faculty of interpretation, or of using words for signs, as completely as he has[*] the faculties of sight and hearing; and words are the means he employs for the exercise of the former faculty, just as the eye and the ear are employed as the organs of the latter.

The power of speech depends on the power of abstraction, *i. e.*, of transforming intuitions into ideas. Let us explain. At the sight of a horse galloping, or of a plain white with snow, the primitive man formed, at first, one undivided image; the motion and the horse, the field and the snow, were unseparated. But, by language, the act of running was distinguished from the creature that ran, and the colour separated from the thing coloured. Each of these two elements became fixed in an isolated word, and so the word dismembered the complete perception. But, from another point of view, the word is more extended than the presentation; *e.g.*, the word "white" expresses not only an attribute of snow, but of all white objects; its meaning, then,

und als dessen Zeichen ihm gleichfalls das Wort dienen muss."— Heyse, *System*, s. 160.

[*] Garnier, *Traité des facultés de l'Âme.* Renan, p. 90.

is more abstract and indeterminate than that of "white snow." Instead of only embracing an existence, or an object in an *accidental* state, a word represents the thing without its accidental characters, which are removed by abstraction, and indicates it under *all* the circumstances in which it may be placed.

The transformation, then, of intuitions into ideas, by the freedom and activity of the human intelligence, constitutes the essence of a word, although the speaker may be as unconscious of the process as he is of the organic mechanisms which give utterance to his thoughts.

I. 'As for the conditions under which articulate language first appeared, M. Steinthal represents them as follows. At the origin of humanity the soul and the body were in such mutual dependence that all the emotions* of the soul had their echo in the body, principally in the organs of the respiration and the voice. This sympathy of soul and body, still found in the infant and the savage, was intimate and fruitful in the primitive man; each intuition awoke in him an accent or

---

* *Motus animi.* In the origin of language, the spontaneous awakening of a sense of the *possibility* of expressing thought by speech, was in point of fact simultaneous with the production of an objective Language as the material in which the awakened intelligence could find expression. Heyse, s. 47.

a sound.' This was the first step; and in this fact
lies the germ of truth contained in the doctrines
of the analogists;[*] since there must have been
some reason in the nature of things, why certain
impressions or feelings were connected with certain sounds rather than with certain others. We
may be totally unable to point out this connection in many cases, and even while recognising
a natural relation between certain sounds of the
human voice and certain material phenomena, we
may deny the very possibility of such a relation between a spiritual phenomenon and its
physical sign. And yet we feel a strong repug-
nance at allowing caprice or chance to have any
considerable share in the origin of language.
It can, at least, be fairly argued that there is
nothing purely arbitrary in the work of the divine
Demiurgus.

II. 'Another law, which played a no less
essential part in the creation of language, was
the association[†] *of ideas.* In virtue of this law,
the sound which accompanied an intuition, asso-
ciated itself in the soul with the intuition itself, so
closely that the sound and the intuition presented

[*] See *ante.*
[†] On this law of association, see Sir W. Hamilton's *Lectures,*
i. 366.

themselves to the consciousness as *inseparable*, and were equally inseparable in the recollection.' This was the second step.

III. Finally, the word became a middle term of reminiscence, a tach between the external object and the inward impression. " The sound* became *a word* by forming a bond between the image obtained by the vision, and the image preserved in the memory; in other words, *it acquired significance, and became an element of language.* The image of the remembrance, and the image of the vision, are not wholly identical; *e.g.*, I see a horse; *no* other horse that I have ever seen resembles it absolutely in colour, size, &c.: the general conception recalled by the word 'horse' involves only the abstracted † attributes common to all the animals of the same genus. It is this collection of common attributes that constitutes the significance of the sound."

Thus M. Steinthal attributes the appearance of language to the unconscious action of psycho-

---

* Exclamations, natural interjections would probably be the first to acquire significance.

† In some savage languages abstraction is at the lowest ebb. Thus, in Iroquois, there is no word for "good" in the abstract, but only words for "a good man," &c. ; and in Mohican there is no verb for "I love," independent of the forms which involve the object of the affection, as "I love him," "I love you."—

logical laws; and as these laws acted spontaneously in the first human beings, it is quite
clear that these speculations involve no approval
of the untenable Epicurean belief in a long period
of mutism and savageness. We cannot but
think that the beauty, ingenuity, and simplicity
of these views will commend them to general
acceptance.

We may here give one or two passing hints of
the way in which these laws were influenced by
organism.

One very simple fact is, that of course the
impressions, &c., which come earliest would naturally be connected with the *sounds* that come
earliest. For instance, the words for father and
mother, which are alike half the world over, are,
as we should have expected, formed of easy and
simple* syllables; being indeed the first labial
sounds of the infant lisping: had we found in

Adelung's *Mithrid.* iii. b. p. 397. So again the Chinese in many
cases cannot express the simple conception without a periphrasis,
and have words for "elder brother" and "younger brother," but
not for "brother."—Humboldt.

* See Gesenius, *Lehrgebäude*, p. 479. Ewald's *Hebrew Grammar*, § 201. "The Mandschou is most like the Semitic here; in
it the origin is still plainer, since *ama* means father, *eme* mother,
according to the uniform distinction of *a* as the stronger, and *e* as
the weaker vowel."—Renan, *Hist. des Langues Sémitiques*, p.
452. Rawlinson's *Herodotus*, i. 481.

any of them the letters which represent late-coming and difficult sounds,* we should have been justly surprised.

Again, Grimm† has remarked that the more ancient a language is, the more clearly do we find in it the distinction between masculine and feminine inflections. "Nothing," adds M. Renan, " proves it more strongly than the to-us-inexplicable tendency which led the primitive nations to suppose a sex in all beings, even inanimate ones. A language, formed in our days, would suppress the gender‡ in all cases, except perhaps, those where men and women are concerned." This peculiarity is doubtless due to the influence of women. In ancient times, the life of woman was far more widely separated than now from that of men; and even in later days, when they were dwarfed in the isolation of the gynæceum, we can easily understand how the peculiarities of their life would have influenced the language they

* Similarly it has been observed by M. Nodier that the most ancient names of God are composed only of the softest and simplest vowels (*Notions*, p. 15). This reminds us of the famous oracle, φράζεο τὸν πάντων ὕπατον θεὸν ἔμμεν' Ἰάω.

† *Uber den Ursprung,* &c., p. 35.

‡ It is strange that the French language should not have adopted the same course as the English, in discarding this useless rag of antiquity. The influences which led to the decision of genders in any particular case were purely fanciful.

employed. The difference between their idioms
and those of men is still very incisive in some
African dialects; and the fact that men in speaking *to* women are obliged to employ particular
inflections, proves that those inflections must have
been used by the women themselves. It is this
which causes the strange difference between Sanskrit and Prâkrit; in the Hindoo dramas, Sanskrit
is used by the men, Prâkrit by the women.

But the difference is *due to the difference of
organisation.* If "a" and "i" are in all languages
the vowels characteristic of the *feminine*, it is
without doubt because those vowels are better
suited to the feminine organ than the masculine
sounds "o" and "ou." A Hindoo commen-
tator, explaining the 10th verse of the Third
book of Manou,* where it is commanded to
give to women sweet and agreeable names,
recommends that in these names the letter "a"
should predominate."

It is observable, too, that the influence of climate on language is in point of fact another
result of the influence of organism. The idiom
of Sybaris is not that of Sparta. The languages of
the South are limpid, euphonic, and harmonious,
as though they had received an impress from the

* Renan, p. 28.

transparency of their heaven, and the soft, sweet sounds of the winds that sigh among their woods. On the other hand, in the hirrients and gutturals, the burr and roughness of the Northern tongues, we catch an echo of the breaker bursting on their crags, and the crashing of the pine-branch over the cataract. Rousseau* has pointed to the fact that the languages of the rich and prodigal South, being the daughters of passion, are poetic and musical, while those of the North, the gloomy daughters of necessity, bear a trace of their hard origin, and express by rude sounds rude sensations. It is an additional argument against the existence of a language primitive, revealed, or innate, that every known language bears on itself the deep traces of predominant local influences. " It is for this reason that the confusion of tongues and the dispersion of nations are represented by Scripture as synchronous events in the magnificent history of Babel, which, perhaps, we may be permitted to regard as one of those sublime parables so frequent in the sacred books. This was the opinion of the great Leibnitz."

These are but easy illustrations of a wide and difficult subject; but the influence of organism

---

* Rousseau, *Essai sur l'Origine des Langues.*

on language has not yet been very fully analysed,
and many of the laws which philologists have
advanced remain to some degree uncertain. Those
who desire to follow the subject may find some
very amusing illustrations in the pages of M.
Nodier, one of which we have* relegated into the
note.

* *Notions,* p. 24 sqq. The remarks on the labials are too
amusing to be omitted. "Le bambin, le poupon, le marmot a
trouvé les trois labiales ; il bée, il baye, il balbutie, il bégaye, il
babille, il blatère, il bêle, il bavarde, il braille, il boude, il bouque,
il bougonne sur une babiole, sur une bagatelle, sur une billevesée,
sur une bêtise, sur un bébé, sur un bonbon, sur un bobo, sur le
bilboquet pendu à l'étalage du bimbelotier. Il nomme sa mère et
son père avec des mimologismes caressants, et quoiqu'il n'ait encore
découvert que la simple touche des lèvres, l'âme se ment déja dans
les mots qu'il module au hasard. Ce Cadmus au maillot vient
d'entrevoir un mystère aussi grand à lui seul que tout le reste de la
création. Il parle sa pensée." Want of space alone compels us to
refrain from transcribing the remarks on the progress of infants
and of society to the dentals. We must say, however, that such
speculations must be very sparingly indulged by sober philologists.
Many of them, at first sight plausible, were refuted by Plato long
ago in the *Cratylus,* and they lead to a grammatical mysticism
which has been well exposed by M. Charma, *Essai,* p. 213.

CHAPTER III.

THE LAWS OF SPECIAL SIGNIFICANCE, OR THE CREATION OF ROOTS.

"Nommer par la mimologie, s'enrichir par la comparaison, les langues n'ont pas d'autre moyen : elles ne sortent pas de là."— Nodier, p. 39.

FROM the general question as to the manner in which sounds acquired significance as *words*, we proceed to the longer and wider inquiry as to the causes which led to the choice of special sounds in special significations; or, in other words, we shall consider the origin of roots.*

When in the first chapter we proved that language was neither innate nor revealed, we proved implicitly that no words could be *purely* arbi-

---

* By roots we do not mean words used in the primitive language, but rather "skeletons of articulate sound." "They are merely the fictions of grammarians to indicate the *core* of a group of related words."—Hensleigh Wedgwood's *Etymolog. Dict.* p. iii. For some remarks on the nature of roots, see Donaldson's *New Cratyl.* bk. iii. ch. 1. Ewald's *Hebrew Gram.* § 202. This naked kernel of a family of words is often best found in the *youngest* dialects, e.g. *kind* (child) from γίγνομαι, genitum, &c.. Grimm, *Deutsche Gramm.* ii. 5. 3. Bopp. *Vgl. Gramm.* s. 131.

trary.* The historic character of language,—the
fact that in innumerable cases we can distinctly
trace the laws which presided at the genesis of any
particular word,—strongly confirms our *à priori*
conclusion. The inference to be deduced from the
labours of all the best philologists, is that of Ihre,
" Non ut fungi nascuntur Vocabula." We have
no reason to believe that any elements of language were deduced from roots which of themselves had no significance; and the more rigorous
and extensive the analysis to which even inflections are subjected, the more clear is the proof
that they arise from the agglutination of separate
and significant words. " We believe," says one
of the ablest of modern† inquirers, " that in
language *ex nihilo nihil fit;* and we are at a loss
to conceive how elements originally destitute of

* One or two philosophers (e.g. Kircher, Becher, Dalgarno,
Bp. Wilkins, Descartes, Leibnitz) have amused themselves with
the invention of languages quite arbitrary, in which every word
was to be accurately determined; but no artificial language
actually used has ever thus arisen. The German *rothwelsch*, the
Italian *gergo*, the French *narquois*, the English "*thieves'* language," the *lingua franca* which serves for commercial purposes
on the shores of the Mediterranean, the strange jargon spoken by
the Chinese and English at Hong Kong, &c., have all arisen from
a corruption of existing languages by metaphors, new words, new
meanings, derivation, composition, &c. See Leibnitz, *Nouv. Essai
sur l'Entendement Humain,* iii. L 2.

† Mr. Garnett, *Essays,* p. 105. Latham, *Lect. on Language.*

signification can determine the sense of anything
with precision.   To assume that they have *no*
meaning, because we cannot always satisfactorily
explain it, is only an *argumentum ad ignoran-
tiam*."

Nor must it be forgotten, that in endeavouring to
prove that in language *nothing is arbitrary*, we are
under a great disadvantage, because no existing
language has come to us in its primitive form.
Every language, even those which are most
ancient, and have long since ceased to be spoken,
bears in its records the traces of a more primitive
condition.   Words, of which the composition was
originally clear, are worn and rubbed by the use
of ages, like the pebbles which are fretted and
rounded into shape and smoothness by the sea
waves on a shingly beach; or to use the more
appropriate image suggested by Goethe, their
meaning is often worn away like the image and
superscription of a coin.   This process is so con-
tinuous, that it is quite hopeless to recover the
original form of many words, or even to make a
probable* guess at their origin.

Language always tends to become mechanical

* What, for instance, is the origin of the initial σ in such words
as σμικρὸς, σφάλλω, or of the initial vowels in ὄνομα, ὀδοὺς,
ἀμίλγω, &c. ?—Garnett, p. 107.

(*i.e.* unmeaning *of itself)* by corruption ;* and to
such an extent is this the case, that it is rather a
matter of astonishment when, after the lapse of
centuries, a word still retains the *obvious* traces
of its original form.   And yet in spite of this we
can by induction discover from words themselves
the *main* laws which influenced the formation of
primitive speech.

The violent dislike which we instinctively feel
to the use of a word entirely new to us, and of
which we do not understand the source, is a
matter of daily experience ; and the tendency to
give a meaning to adopted words by so changing
them as to remove their seemingly *arbitrary*
character has exercised a permanent and appre-
ciable influence on every language.   An instance
or two will perhaps pave the way for a more
ready acceptance of our subsequent remarks.

When we go into a ship or factory, and inquire the
technical name of various parts of the machinery,
we are either unable to use the names from not

---

* When a boy answers a lady in the words " Yes, 'm," he is
not aware that his "'m" is a fragment of the five syllables
mea domina (madonna, madame, madam, ma'am, 'm.)   " Letters,
like soldiers, being very apt to desert and drop off in a long
march."—*Divers. of Purley*, pt. i. ch. vi.   "Les noms des saints
et les noms des baptêmes les plus communs en sont un exemple."—
De Brosses.

catching the pronunciation, or, in attempting to pronounce them we substitute for them other words of similar sound and more significance.

It often happens that gardeners become acquainted with new plants, or new species of old plants, that are brought to them under a foreign name; not understanding this name, they corrupt it into some word which sounds like it, and with which they are already familiar. To this source of corruption we owe such words as dandylion* (*dent de lion*), rosemary (*ros marinus*), gilly-flower (*girofle*), quarter sessions rose (*des quatre saisons*), Jerusalem artichoke (*giresol*) &c. For the same reason (the dislike of terms with which they are unacquainted) sailors corrupt Bellerophon into Billy Ruffian: and we have heard of a groom, who, having the charge of two horses called Othello and Desdemona, christened them respectively Old Fellow and Thursday Morning. Lamprocles, the name of a horse of Lord Eglintoun's, was converted by the ring into "Lamb and Pickles." The same principle may be seen at work among servants; we have heard a servant systematically use the word "cravat" for "carafe," and astonish a gentleman by calmly

* See *Philological Transactions*, v. 133 sq.

asking him at luncheon, "If she should fill his *cravat* with water?"

The working of this tendency is all the more curious from the fact that very often the corrupted form of the word is wholly *inappropriate*, although significant.   There is no doubt that, in most cases, we prefer a corruption, which is appropriate *as well as* significant, and we find instances* of· this in such words as wormwood (*wermuth*), cray-*fish* (*écrévisse*), lant*horn* (*laterna*), belfry (*beffroi*), rake*hell* (*racaille*), beefeater (*buffetier*), verdi*grease* (*verd de gris*), sparrow-*grass* (asparagus), &c.   Where, however, this is unattainable, we are well content with some significant corruption, for which we can invent or imagine a meaning even if we are unaware of the real explanation ; as, for instance, in Charter House (*Chartreuse*), "to a cow's thumb"= exactly (*à la coutume*), wiseacre (*weissager*), saltpetre (*salpetra*), &c.   It is curious to find that in the desire to understand, at any rate in *some* degree, the words we use, the corrupted form

---

* *Phil. Trans.* v. 133 sq.   "The facility with which unusual or difficult words are corrupted is being at this moment strikingly illustrated in the numerous Spanish words introduced into our language through the American conquests in Mexico ;   cañon, stancia, stampedo, &c., are already altered in form."—R. G.

often gives birth to a totally false explanation.
Thus Dr. Latham mentions * that the corruption of
Château Vert into Shotover has led to the legend
that Little John *shot over* the hill of that name
near Oxford. Similar instances are supplied by
the legends of Veronica, and of St. Ursula with
her *eleven thousand* virgins.

It may seem that we have, in the course of this
chapter, made statements somewhat contradictory ; viz., that it is the tendency of language to become mechanical (*i. e.*, arbitrary and conventional)
by corruption, and yet that there is an instinctive dislike to the use of new words which convey
no intrinsic meaning to the mind of the speaker.
If we argued from the instances adduced in the
last pages, we *might* infer that language was

---

* *Engl. Lang.* i. p. 356, 4th ed. St. Aldhelm's Head, in Dorset-
shire, is always pronounced and generally written St. Alban's Head,
although St. Alban had no connection with it. Penny-come-quick
was a very natural corruption of Pen, Coombe, and Ick, the former
name for Falmouth. These words form a curious chapter in the
history of language. There is no doubt that the mythological
legends of a later period are largely suggested by the corruption of
names, as in the case of *Aphrodite, Dionysus,* &c. The fiction of
an Oriental nation provided with a two-fold tongue (Diod. Sic. ii.)
might easily spring from the word δίγλωσσος. See many such
instances in Lersch. iii. 6 fg. The Greek 'Ιεροσόλυμα presents a
double instance of this, being corrupted from ירושלים, which is
itself probably a corruption of the old Canaanite name for
Jerusalem. *Dict. of Bibl. Ant.* s. v.

originally arbitrary, and had been twisted into
meaning by subsequent use. We must, however,
draw attention to the fact that this latter phenomenon is only observable on the naturalisation
of a word. A new word, however bright and
perfect in itself, is like a strange coin upon which
we look with suspicion, because we are unaccustomed to its appearance. But when a word
is accepted and generally understood, when, in
fact, it has *become current*, we are then indifferent
to the amount of wear on the surface or even to
the complete obliteration of its original significance ; just in the same way as we do not trouble
ourselves to observe a coin which is in common
use, and pay no regard to the fact that its image
is confused, and its superscription undecipher-
able. We might, for instance, find words which
have passed through both processes. Let us
suppose * that, in course of time, the word *sherbet*
had become corrupted first into *syrup*, then into
shrub ; in this case we should have an exemplification of a word first appropriately corrupted into
a familiar form in the course of naturalisation,
and then re-corrupted into a purely mechanical †

* The instance is a pure supposition, for sherbet, syrup, and
shrub are from the same Arabic root, coming to us from three
different sources.—Latham.

† We know of very few words *invented* on simply arbitrary

word, by the ordinary progress of language. We are therefore fairly entitled to infer from the dislike to the introduction of any sound as a word, when the sound is to the speaker an arbitrary one, that the same feeling must have operated at the dawning exercise of the faculty of speech; while from the indifference which we exhibit to the corruption of a word when it has once been currently received, we may give a reason for our inability to explain the origin of *all* primitive roots, even while we assume with confidence that every root was originally significative.

grounds. "Sepals" was devised by Neckar to express each division of the calyx (Whewell, *Hist. Ind. Sc.* ii. 535), and yet we see at once that it is only a very slight alteration of the word "petals," and this no doubt was the reason, not only for the choice of it, but also for the ready currency which it obtained. The term "Od force" is another instance. Chemistry at one period affected to give to simple bodies only such names as were destitute of all significance; but it abandoned this practice in consequence of the absurdities and impossibilities which it involved. (v. Renan, p. 148.) Thus, "*sulfite*" and "*sulfate*" are due to Guyton de Morveau. (Charma, p. 66.) "*Ellagic*" acid is the name given by M. Draconnot to the substance left in the process of making pyrogallic acid, and it is derived from Galle read backwards (*Hist. Ind. Sc.* ii. 547); but such terms are justly reprobated by men of science. Even proper names, which some have supposed to be often arbitrary, are in almost every case found capable of a real etymology. "Ils n'ont pas, plus que les autres mots, été imposés sans *cause*, ni fabriqués *au hasard*, seulement pour produire une bruit vague."—De Brosses. This was noticed very early; see *Schol. ad Hom. Od.* xix. 406.

Language may be regarded as the union of
words and grammar, of which words are analogous to matter, and grammar to form ;* regarded
in its *form* it was the expression of pure reason ;
in its *matter* it was only the reflex of sensuous
life. The absence of any definite grammar constitutes an *inorganic* language like the Chinese.
Those who have derived language exclusively from
sensation are as much mistaken as those who
have assigned to ideas a purely material origin.
Sensation furnished the variable and accidental
element, which might have been quite other than
it is, (*i. e.*, the words); but the grammar of a
language, (the rational form, without which words
could not have been a language), is its pure and
transcendental element which gives to the result
its truly human character. Words can no more
form a language than sensations can produce a
man. That which originates language, like that
which originates thought, is the logical relation
which the soul establishes between external
things.

We may now state our belief that *almost all*
primitive roots were obtained by *Onomatopœia*,
i. e., by an imitation with the human voice of
the sounds of inanimate nature. Onomatopœia

* Renan, p. 122.

sufficed to represent the vast majority of physical
facts and external phenomena; and nearly all the
words requisite for the expression of metaphysical
and moral convictions were derived from these*
onomatopœic roots by *analogy* and *metaphor.*

We have purposely modified our statement of
these conclusions, because there is too great a
tendency to general assertions, against which, as
W. von Humboldt well remarked, science should
be always on its guard. It is a saying of
Schlegel's, that, so great is the variety of procedure in different languages, that there is
scarcely one language which might not be chosen
to illustrate some particular hypothesis. For
instance, the *sole* similarity between Chinese and
Sanskrit rests in the fact that both aim at the
same end, viz., the expression of thought. Thus
onomatopœia is far from being found in all languages in the same degree, and it is much more
observable in the Semitic than in the Indo-
European family, in which, however ancient the
word may be proved to be, it constantly bears
witness to those poetic and philosophic instincts
of our race which clearly prove that reason was
not a slow and painful growth.

" Caprice has no influence in the formation of

* Nodier, p. 39. See, too, Garnett's *Essays*, p. 89.

language." Without believing in any universal,
necessary, intrinsic connection between word
and thing, we are forced to believe that there was,
in every case, a *subjective* connection. The appropriateness of the word resided, not in the object
named, for in this case there would have been a
striking similarity in all the languages of the
human race, but in the mind of the name-giver,
who, of necessity, stamped the word with the
impress of his own individuality. In direct
proportion to the delicacy of his perceptions, was
the fitness of the words he used ; for those words
expressed relations capable of being viewed in
widely different aspects, so that the finer and
more keen was the man's power of perceiving
analogies, the greater was his capacity for the
expression of facts. The true formula is that
"the connection between a word and its meaning is never *necessary*, and never arbitrary, but
always results from a reasonable motive."

But what the motives were, which in many
cases led to the choice of particular sounds, it is
beyond our power to conjecture or ascertain.
The richness and delicacy of the appellative
faculty in the savage and the infant must necessarily have existed in the primitive man, and, as
it decayed with the decay of all necessity for its

exercise, we are unable to point out, with any
certainty, the tendencies by which it was actuated.
There is no waste in the economy of nature ; a
faculty ceases when it is no longer required, just
as the outer leaves which ensheathe the nascent
germ wither and drop off when the germ has
acquired sufficient vitality for its own preservation.

"Tecum habita" was not the motto of the
early inhabitants of the earth. They lived with
the external world. The cataract "haunted them
like a passion," and they heard voices in the
dawning of the sun and the murmur of the
wind. The heavens declared the glory of God,
and the firmament showed his handiwork; day
unto day uttered speech, and night showed knowledge unto night. The soul of the first man, to
use the beautiful expression of Leibnitz, was a
concentric mirror of nature, in the midst of
whose works he lived. Language was the echo
of nature in his individual consciousness. The
action of the mind produced language by a
spontaneous repercussion of the perceptions
received.[*] It is the mind which creates and forms ;
but this power of the mind is one reacting only
upon impressions received from the world with-

* Bunsen, *Outlines*, s. ii. 84. 78.

out. The imitative power of language consists in an artistic imitation, not of things, but of the rational impression which an object produces by its qualities.

The fact, therefore, that the imitation is *artistic*, and is influenced by subjective considerations, would prevent us from being surprised or disappointed, if we do not always see the working of this principle, in cases where we should have expected it. In such words as the Hebrew *Khátzatz* (קָצַץ), and *Schephifoun* (שְׁפִיפוֹן) we seem to hear the shearing off of the cut material, and the lithe rustle of the horned snake through the withered leaves. But words so remarkably suggestive are comparatively rare, and in most cases the imitation is more concealed. Nothing, however, more powerfully proves the tendency of language, in this respect, than the fact that words of a harsh meaning usually assume a rough, harsh form, and words that imply something sweet and tender seem to breathe the sensation they describe. The German word (entsetzen) "terror," means, etymologically, a mere "displacement," yet who does not see that it has caught an instinctive echo from the thing which it describes, which, in no degree, depends on association;— that, independently of imagination it betrays something harsh by its mere form. That there is a consonance between external sounds and the processes of the mind, is decisively shown by the fact that whole languages have thus caught the impress of the associations by which they have been evolved. In the soft and vowelled undersong of modern Italian, who does not recognise the result of climate and natural character? The Doric seems to recall to us the sound of martial flutes, while the Hebrew, in its stern and solemn pomp, tells like one vast onomatopœia, of the mighty mission which it was destined to accomplish; every single word of it seems to shine with that mysterious light which lent strange lustre to the letters of it on the gems of the sacerdotal robe. "When," says M. Vinet, "you hear the vast word haschâmaïm, which names the heavens, unfold itself like a vast pavilion, your intelligence—before knowing what the word signifies—expects something magnificent; no mean object could have been named thus; it is better than an onomatopœia, although it is not one." *

The exuberance and uncontrolled variety

* *Essais de Phil. Morale*, p. 344. (The word שָׁמַיִם comes from a root signifying height.) Several of the instances in this paragraph are from M. Vinet.

which characterises the primitive languages is a
proof of the extraordinarily developed resources
of the power of interpretation, or the faculty of
converting sounds into signs, so long as the
exercise of that faculty continued to be necessary.
The richest idioms are always the most spontaneous and unconscious. It is obviously impossible for us, with our intellectual refinements
and blunted senses, to rediscover the ancient
harmony which existed between thought and
sensation, between nature and man. As we are
no longer obliged to create language, we have
entirely lost a crowd of processes which tended
to its elaboration. But among the early races
there was a delicate tact, enabling them to seize
on those attributes which were capable of supplying them with appellatives, the exquisite subtlety
of which we are unable any longer to conceive.*
They saw a thousand things at once, and indeed
their language-creating faculty mainly consisted
in a power of seizing upon relations. Our very
civilisation has robbed us of this happy and
audacious power. Nature spoke more to them
than to us, or rather they found in themselves a

* "Augustus himself, in the possession of that power which
ruled the world, acknowledged that he could not make a new Latin
word."—Locke, iii. 2. 8.

secret echo which answered to all external voices, and returned them in articulations—in *words*. Hence those swift interchanges of meaning which we, with our less flashing intelligence, are almost unable to follow.[*] 'Who can seize again those fugitive impressions of the naïfs creators of language in words which have undergone so many changes, and which are so far from their original acceptation? Who can rediscover the capricious paths which the imagination followed, and the associations of ideas which guided it, in that spontaneous work, wherein sometimes man, sometimes nature, reunited the broken thread of analogies, and wove their reciprocal actions into an indissoluble unity?'

Wherever the faculty of creating appellations is still required, we still find a capacity for its exercise. For instance, it has been asserted that "the day after an army has encamped in an unknown country all the important or charac-

---

[*] Renan, p. 143. "Though the origin of most of our words is forgotten, each word was at first a stroke of genius, and obtained currency, because for the moment it symbolised the world to the speaker and the hearer. . . . As the limestone of the Continent consists of infinite masses of the shells of animalcules, so language is made up of images and tropes, which now in their secondary use have long ceased to remind us of their poetic origin."—Emerson, *Ess. on the Poet.*

teristic places have their names without any convention having intervened." We find an analogous
case in the fact that the French and English, by
common consent, called the Turks Bono Johnny;
the exact reasons for such a nomenclature would
be perhaps difficult to determine, and who shall
say who first used or invented the term? yet it
became current in a day or two. It is equally
difficult to trace the history and origin of various
popular phrases which every now and then have a
brief run in ordinary phraseology.

A still more remarkable exemplification that
the faculty of the original name-giver is not
wholly lost to mankind may be seen in the secret,
subtle, almost imperceptible, and sometimes
quite unconscious analogies which give currency
to a common nickname. At schools I have often
known boys whose sobriquet was a vocable, in
itself apparently meaningless and incapable of
any circumstantial explanation, which was yet
universally adopted, and was adopted *because* it
presented some unintelligible appropriateness.*

* Take, for instance, the word "fal-lala," borrowed from the
burden of a song, and often used to describe female vanities. Does
not this word afford a curious analogy to the word "falbala," the
origin of which (to express similar articles) has occupied the
attention of distinguished philosophers? It has been explained as
follows. It is said that a witty prince of the eighteenth century

A modern prince is called Plomb-plomb, and
known quite commonly by that designation : yet
there is no such word as Plomb-plomb in the
French language, and the very origin of the term
is unknown to the majority of the Prince's con-
temporaries. We may be quite sure, however,
that the name involves either a lively onomatopœia
or a striking allusion.*

once entered an elegant shop, and determined to try to the utmost
the assurance of the (probably pretty) milliner. He therefore
asked for a *falbala*, inventing the oddest vocable he could think
of. With admirable but unconscious insight into the principle
of language, the undisturbed female at once brought him the
garniture de robe called volant, which ended in light floating
points. She instinctively caught the notion involved in flabella,
flammula, &c.—Nodier, p. 211. The story is told differently by
De Brosses, *Form Méch.* ch. xvi. § 14. The word has excited
much discussion. Leibnitz connects it with *fald-plat*, and
Hoffman with *furbelow.* Charma, p. 306. The murderer, Pierre
Rivière, invented the word *ennepharer* for the torture to which he
used, when a boy, to subject frogs ; and the word *calibène* for the
instrument which he constructed to kill birds. Charma, p. 66.
Du Mérit notices the purely musical names which children
instinctively give to those who inspire them with strongly marked
feelings of love. "Rumpelstiltskin," the name of the imp in the
fairy tale, is a good instance of the reverse.

* It is mainly among the people, rather than with philosophers,
that the power of inventing names has lingered. Some write the
name Plonplon, and make it a familiar abbreviation of Napoleon ;
but accomplished Frenchmen give differing accounts of the word.

CHAPTER IV.

ONOMATOPŒIA.*

"The sound must seem an echo to the sense."—POPE.

SINCE the human voice is at once a *sound* and
a *sign*, it was of course natural to take the sound
of the voice as a sign of the sounds of nature.†
In short, to recall a sound by its echo in the voice
is as obviously natural a proceeding as to recall
an object to the memory by drawing the picture
of its form. In both cases we act upon the senses
by means of imitation ; and if the human race
had not been endued with the organs of hearing
doubtless a language for the eye would have been
invented, just as Philomela, when deprived of
her tongue, made known, by embroidery, her

---

* Ὄνομα ποιέω. "Ὀνοματοποιΐα est dictio ad imitandum sonum
vocis conficta, ut cum dicimus *hinnire* equos, *balare* oves, *stridere*
valvas." Charis. iv. p. 245. Lersch, i. 129—232. The Latins
call it "fictio nominis."

† Renan, p. 136. We have already endeavoured to guard
against the misconception that language is in any sense a *result* of
imitation : a mere power of imitating the sounds of nature belongs
to animals as well as to man.—Heyse, s. 91, and supra ch. i.

miserable tale. A word formed on the principle of imitation, is said to be formed by onomatopœia, and although the traces of such an origin are rapidly lost, yet amid the almost infinite modifications of which a few roots are capable, it is astonishing how vast a number of words may be ultimately deduced from a single onomatopœic sound.

How universal and instinctive the procedure is, may be observed among infants and savages.

In the nursery the onomatopœan sounds moo, baa, bow-wow, &c., are the steps by which the child passes gradually to the conception of cow, lamb, and dog. So in Swiss* bàùgen is to bleat, and báágeli (in nursery language), a sheep. The very name *cow*, Germ. *kuh*, Sansks. *gao*, has a similar origin, as βοῦς, bos, ox, Sansks. uxan, probably has also. There is little doubt that the word, cat (Germ. *katze*), is an imitation of the sound made by a cat spitting, which is one of the most peculiar characteristics of the feline race. It must, however, be admitted that there is no sibilant in "kater." We have all heard the story

---

* Wedgwood's *Etym. Dict.* p. v. It is necessary to be cautious, of course, in deducing the processes of language from the observation of children. See Heyse, s. 47. The word moo-cow is a mixture of pure onomatopœia, and onomatopœia after it has become conventional.

of the Englishman in China, who, wishing to
know the contents of a dish which was lying
before him, said inquiringly, " Quack, quack ? "
and received in answer, the word, " bow-wow ! "
These two imitations served all the purposes of a
more lengthened conversation. It was probably,
by a strictly analogous process, that an immense
multitude of such roots was primitively formed.

Again, it is impossible to look over any list of
words collected from the language of a savage
community without recognising the extensive use
of the same method.* The repetition of syllables
is an almost certain sign of its working. Thus,
Ai-ai is an imitation of the cry of the sloth, and
tuco-tuco is the name of a small rodent in Buenos
Ayres. Mr. Longfellow has supplied us with
many such words from the languages of North
America, in his poem of " Hiawatha,"—as Kah-
gahgee, the raven ; Minnehaha laughing-water,
&c. " In uncivilised languages," the consciousness of the imitative character of certain words is
sometimes demonstrated by their composition
with verbs,† like say or do, to signify making a
noise like that represented by the word in question. Thus, in Galla, from *djeda*, to say, or *goda*,

* See the lists of such vocabularies in the *Transactions of the
Philol. Soc.*   † Wedgwood, p. v.

to make or do, are formed *cacak-djeda*, to crack;
trrr-djeda, to chirp; *dadada-djeda*, to beat; *djam-
djam-goda*, to champ."

We do not think that the extent to which onomatopœia may be proved to be an instrument of
language has been sufficiently admitted. It was the
most natural starting-point for the intelligence on
its path towards expression. A nascent language
enriches itself by ceaseless imitations of elementary sounds, animal cries, and the noises
produced by mechanical contrivances, and we
shall trace hereafter the innumerable applications
in which such terms can be at once employed.
Some writers even go so far as to assert that
this is the *only* original principle of language,
and that we even learned our first consonant from
the bleating of the sheep, for which reason,
according to Pierius Valerianus, a lamb was the
hieroglyphical emblem of the verb! We have
already rejected this extension of the theory; but,
at the same time, we can readily believe the
assertion, that the *peculiarities* of articulation in
certain countries may be not only modified, but
even originated by the existence of remarkable
natural sounds in the countries where these peculiarities occur. It has been said, for instance,
" that in some of the American languages, there

are strident consonants evidently formed from
the hiss of certain serpents unknown in our
temperate regions, and that the click of the
Hottentot dialects recalls a species of cry peculiar
to the tigers which *ranque.*"   The latter word is
an onomatopœian, probably borrowed by Buffon
from the Philomela of Albus Ovidius Juventinus,
in which occurs the line :—

"Tigrides indomitæ *rancant** rugiuntque leonea."

What this peculiar sound may be, we do not
know, but can hardly reconcile this suggestion of
Nodier with the statement, that the name,† Hott-
en-tot is itself onomatopœian, having been given
by the first Dutch settlers, because this click
would sound to a stranger like a perpetual
repetition of the syllables *hot* and *tot.*   It is a
curious fact that Palamedes is said to have learnt,
from the noise of cranes, the four letters which
he added to the Greek alphabet; and it is certainly
a confirmation of these remarks, that although no
language possesses in its alphabet a power of
expressing every possible articulation, yet no
nation's language is quite deficient in the power

* L. 45. "Proprium tigridis, a sono. Alii leg. *raucant*."—
Forcellini, *Lex.*
† Wedgwood, p. vi. The name is not native probably, for the
native tribe-names mostly end in qua ; as Griqua, Namaqua, &c.

of expressing, by imitation, the cries of its indigenous animals.

It is wonderful that the knowledge and observation of facts like these did not lead the philologists of antiquity to a solution of their disputes about the natural or conventional origin cf languages. The age of Psammetichus evinced its interest in the question, and if it had been content to observe its own experiment, instead of making it the prop to a "foregone conclusion," philosophers might have agreed, long ago, in believing, that man was assisted by nature in the development of his implanted powers, and that, like every infant of his race, he framed into living speech the sounds by which his senses were first impressed.* When the first man gave names to the animals, which, as we have already seen, he was enabled to do by the reasonable use of his own faculties, and not at the dictation of a voice from heaven, he could not have been guided by *any* principle so obvious, so easy, or so appropriate as an artistic reproduction of the sounds which they uttered.

But how, it may be asked, is the voice capable

* Nodier, p. 79 seq. Dr. Pickering quotes an account of the *original people* of Malay, in which it is said that "their language is not understood by any one : they lisp their words, *the sound of which is like the noise of birds.*" (*Races of Man*. Bohn ed. p. 305.)

of rendering even the feeblest echo of all the
myriad utterances of the earth and air, the voices
of the desert and mountain,—

> " The echoes of illimitable forests,
> The murmur of unfathomable seas" !

We answer that the imitation is not, and does
not profess to be a dull, dead, passive echo of
the *sound*, but of the impression produced by it
upon the sentient being; it is not a *mere* spontaneous repercussion of the perception received;
but a repercussion modified *organically* by the
configurations of the mouth, and *ideally* by the
nature of the analogy perceived between the
sound and the object it expressed. " The organs
of that wonderful musical instrument, the mouth,
are the throat, the palate, the tongue, the teeth,
the lips.* This then is the subjective organon of
language, the physiological vehicle for that proto-
plastic art, speech, which combines architecture
and music, the plastic and the picturesque.
Johannes Müller has developed this physiologi-

---

* Bunsen, *Outlines*, ii. 82. The poet Shelley implied the same
thought in *Alastor*:

> " I wait breath, Great Parent, that my song
> May *modulate* with motions of the air,
> And murmurs of the forest and the sea,
> And voice of living beings, and woven hymns
> Of night and day, and *the deep heart of man.*"

cally, Sir John Herschell acoustically." The
mere power of imitation would not have helped
mankind a single step towards language any more
than it has helped the parrot or the jay,* had it
not been for the infinitely nobler faculty which
enabled us to perceive the meaning of the sounds
we uttered, and to use them as the signs of our
inward conceptions,—a faculty which has implanted in language its principle of development,
and which constitutes the distinction between the
chatterings of a jackdaw and the eloquence of
a man.

This alone is a clear proof, if proof were wanted,
that language is the result of intelligence, as well
as of instinct ; and that the human reason was not
a gradual acquisition of a once brutish race.

But though the power of imitation by the voice
of the sounds of the unintelligent creation be
small in comparison with those other powers
which constitute our pre-eminence, yet how perfect is that gift in itself,—how wondrous the
organism by which it is effected! The mouth is
admirably framed for intelligent and harmonious
utterance ; it is at once an organ, and a flute,—a
trumpet and a harp. Its sublime construction
will make it the eternal despair of mechanicians,

* Locke *on the Human Understanding*, iii. i. § 1, 2.

and the songs which it can modulate, are superior to all the melodies of artificial music. The intelligence of man enables him alone to use this glorious instrument, as God intended it to be used. "Il avait," says M. Nodier, "dans ses poumons un soufflet intelligent et sensible, dans ses lèvres un limbe épanoui, mobile, extensible, rétractile, qui jette le son, qui le modifie, qui le renforce, qui l'assouplit, qui le contraint, qui le voile, qui l'éteint; dans sa langue un marteau souple, flexible, onduleux, qui se replit, qui s'accourcit, qui s'étend; qui se meut, et qui s'enterpose entre ses valves, selon qu'il convient retenir ou d'épancher la voix, qui attache ses touches avec âpreté ou qui les effleure avec mollesse; dans ses dents un clavier ferme, aigu, strident; à son palais un tympan grave et sonore: luxe inutile pourtant, s'il n'avait pas eu la pensée; et celui qui a fait ce qui est n'a jamais rien fait d'inutile.—L'homme parla parce qu'il pensait."

The plain elementary sounds of which the human voice is capable are about twenty; and yet it has been calculated by the mathematician Tacquet, that one thousand million writers, in one thousand million years, could not write out all the combinations of the twenty-four letters of the alphabet, if each of them were daily to write

out forty pages of them, of which each page
should contain different orders of the twenty-
four letters. Of course, a very small number only
of these permutations are at all required for every
purpose of life. " And thus it is," says the ingenious author of *Hermes, " that to principles
apparently so trivial as about twenty plain
elementary sounds, we owe that variety of articulate voices, which have been sufficient to explain
the sentiments of so innumerable a multitude, as
all the present and past generations of men."

But it may be objected that if we admit such
latitude to the use of onomatopœia in the formation of language, we should find among all languages a much greater identity than actually
exists in the terms expressive of physical facts.
This by no means follows. We have already
seen that words express the *relations* of things,
and the relations of things are almost infinite,
and especially must they have been so to the
delicate senses of the youthful world. Let us
take the instance of the thunder : the impression
produced by it is by no means single and distinct.
To one man it may appear like a dull rumble, to
another like a sudden crackling explosion, and to
a third as a breaking forth of flashing light.

* Harris's *Hermes*, bk. ii. ch. 2, 3rd ed. p. 325.

Hence come a multitude of names. Adelung professed to have collected 353 imitative appellations from the European languages alone; and it is not difficult to see that a similar* principle was at work in the Chinese *ley* (pronounced *rey*), the Greenland *kallak*, and the Mexican *tlatlatnitzel*. Similarly, " the explosion of a gun which an English boy imitates by the exclamation *Bang-fire*, is represented in French by *Pouf!* The neighing of a horse is expressed by the French *hennir;* Italian, *nitrire;* Spanish, *rinchar, relinchar;* German, *wiehern;* Swedish, *wrena, wrenska;* Dutch, *runniken, ginniken, brieschen*, words in which it is difficult to see a glimpse of resemblance, although we can hardly doubt that they all take their rise in the attempt at direct† repre-

---

* Renan, p. 139, quoting Adelung, *Mithrid.* i. p. xiv. Grimm, *Über die Namen des Donners.* (Berlin, .1855.) If the words "tonitru," "donner," &c., be not originally onomatopœian, as some assert (who derive them from *tan*, Gr. τείνειν), they *became* so from a feeling of the need that they should be.—Heyse, s. 93.

† Wedgwood, p. 5. The word "pouf" is also used of falling bodies, as in the Macaronic verse, "De brancha in brancham degringolat atque facit '*pouf*.'" It would be interesting to trace the causes for the divergencies in sound of obvious onomatopœian words in various languages : e. g. It is clear that "ding-dong" could only be used to denote the sound of a bell in a country possessing large heavy bells, and therefore churches. The sound *bil* or bell (Cf. tintinnabulum), expressive of a clear sharp tinkle, would naturally be used by a people, like the Galla, only accustomed

sentation of the same sound." In the same way, no one will deny that " ding-dong," and the word " bilbil," to ring, in the Galla language, are onomatopœians to represent the sound of a bell, and yet the two have hardly an element in common.

It has been noticed that birds are often named on this principle ; as night-jar, whip-poor-will, cock, cuckoo, crow, crane, crake, quail, curlew, jay, chough, owl, turtle, &c. ; and where the bird has one very marked cry we find a great similarity in the names by which it is known. Take for instance the *peewit*," Scandinavian *pee-weip, tee-whoap;* French, *dishuit;* Dutch, *kiewit*; German, *kiebitz;* Swedish, *kowipa.* But we should not expect this to be the case when a bird has a great variety of different sounds. The nightingale, according to Bechstein, has twenty distinct articulations, and it is therefore not surprising that even in the European languages it is known under widely different names. And besides names which are derived from its song (*e. g.* bulbul), it might be called from some other attri-

to the small bells sold as trinkets by foreign traders. Among the Suaheli languages (out of five words given in Krapf's vocabulary), no word for a bell at all resembles the sound. I am indebted to my friend, Mr. Garnett, for these remarks, as well as for other ingenious suggestions.　　　* Wedgwood, *Etymol. Dict.*

84 AN ESSAY ON

bute entirely distinct from this, as perhaps in
the Latin name *luscinia;* although, if this be the
case, it is interesting to see how imitation asserts
its prerogative in the modern names* *usig-
nuolo* (Italian), *ruyseñol* (Spanish), *rossignol*
(French), *rousinol* (Portuguese), which are probably corruptions of the diminutive *lusciniola,*
used by Plautus.

In some cases an onomatopœian root is so natural as to run through all families of languages;
e. g. the root lh or lk to imitate the sound and
action of licking, as Hebrew לְחַךְ; Arabic, *lahika;*
Syriac, *lah;* λείχω, *lingo, ligurio, lingua, leccare,
lechen, lécher;* it is the same with the roots grf
to express gripping, kr to express crying, and
many others. The practice is, however (as

* Nodier, p. 41. Even when the sound is no guide, *different*
characteristics are chosen by different nations to furnish a name.
The names "*fledermaus*," "*flittermouse*," are suggested like
"*chauve souris*," by the structure of the bat; νυκτερίς and
vespertilio by its habits; if the differentia of the animal be *very*
marked, its name will probably be derived from it in all languages,
as *noctiluca, glow*-worm, *lucciolato,* ver *luisant,* &c.; yet even
then not in all, as *Johannis-wurm.* Compare again σεισουργίς,
motacilla, cutretta, wagtail, with *Bachstelze, hoche-queue,* &c. If
the bird be rare, it is much more likely to have numerous names,
because the observation of each casual observer as to its chief
attribute is not liable to so much revision. Take as an instance
the night-jar, which is also called fern-owl, churn-owl, goat-sucker,
a beel-bird, dorhawk, &c. See, too, Garnett's *Essays,* pp. 88, 89.

we have already remarked), far more prominent
in the Semitic than in the Indo-European family,
and this is the cause of the extraordinary richness
of synonyms in Hebrew and Arabic for the expression of natural objects. It is said that in
Arabic there are 500 names for the lion, 200 for
the serpent, more than eighty for honey, 400 for
sorrow, and (what is quite incredible unless
every periphrasis be counted a name) no less
than 1,000 for a sword.   M. de Hammer, an un-
impeachable authority, has, in a little treatise on
the subject, counted also 5,744 words relating to
the camel. The ancient Saxon is said to have
had fifteen words for the sea; and if we allowed
merely poetical expressions like "the blue," we
might say the same of modern English.

Wide dialectic variety naturally results from a
nomadic life; and it is easy to see how this
extraordinary exuberance of primitive language,
and the uncontrolled rapidity with which it exercised its powers of nomenclature, would tend,
while writing and literature were as yet unknown, to make mutually unintelligible the lan-·
guage of different tribes.*   This confusion of

* "The *physiognomy*, however, of a group of languages remains
unaffected by the divergency of their vocabularies; e.g. almost
every word in the Ethiopic family of languages contains a liquid

speech would, of course, be the most powerful
impediment in the course of ambition, and
would tend to defeat the attempts to construct
and perpetuate a universal empire. It may have
been the providential agent to assert for the
human race, " a nobler destiny than to become
the footstool of a few families." This is strikingly shadowed forth in the Scripture narrative
of the builders of Babel, which many competent
authorities have considered as applicable to only
a single family of nations, and have regarded in
the light rather of " a sublime emblem, than of a
material verity."

The confusion of tongues is not represented
in Scripture as a punishment,* but as the providential prevention of an arrogant attempt to
establish among mankind a spurious centre of
unity. It seems to have frustrated the lawless
thirst for power which actuated the tribe of Nim-
rod.† But even if regarded as a punishment,

generally in connection with a mute as its most prominent and
essential feature."—R. G.

* It is represented as a punishment in some legends, as in the
fragment of Abydenus, &c., quoted by Euseb. *Præp. Ev.* ix. 14.
Joseph. *Antt.* i. iv. 3. Plat. *Polit.* p. 272. Plin. vii. 1. xi. 112.
But see Abbt's Dissertation, "*Confusionem linguarum non fuisse
pœnam humano generi inflictam.*" Hal. 1753.

† καὶ περίστα δὲ κατ᾽ ὀλίγον εἰς τυραννίδα τὰ πράγματα.—
Joseph. *Antt.* i. iv. 2.

God's punishments are but blessings in disguise. The dispersion of nations has acted as a stimulant to the powers of humanity, and has been the direct cause of a beneficial variety in thought and action ; and in the same way the diversity of languages has proved to be (as we shall see hereafter) an indisputable advantage, by adding fresh lustre continually to those conceptions which by long habit become pale and dim.   Yet this dispersion and diversity is but the accident of a fallen state, and in the renovated earth—(though it can never be while nations are in their present condition)—all men will perhaps speak the same perfect* universal speech.

There are two totally distinct points from which an imitative root can take its origin.   The first is from an artistic reproduction of the sounds of the outer world ; the second is from the expressions of fear or anger, of disgust or joy, which the impression of any event or spectacle may call forth in the human being.   The first of these elements is the onomatopœic ; the second, the interjectional.   These two sources have not been kept sufficiently clear and distinct, and the latter especially has been by many philologists entirely overlooked.   We will proceed to make

* 1 Cor. xiii. 8 ; Rev. vii. 9 ; Zach. viii. 23 ; Zeph. 9, &c.

some remarks on both. The instances which we
shall select might be almost indefinitely extended,
and even were they less numerous we might
perhaps be allowed to use the words of President
de Brosses, "La preuve connue d'un grand
nombre de mots d'une espèce doit établir une
précepte générale sur les autres mots de même
espèce, à l'origine desquels on ne peut plus
remonter."

As instances of the words which have arisen
from the interjectional element, *i. e.* from the
sounds whereby we express natural emotions, we
may mention the large group of words that spring
from the root "ach," ah! oh! as utterances of
pain, as ἄχος, ἀχέω, *achen*, ache; or from the
sound of groaning, as *væ*, *wehe*, woe, wail; or
from an expression of disgust, as *putere* (Fr.
puer), foul, fulsome; or from smacking the lips
with pleasure, as γλύκυς, *dulcis*, *geschmack*, &c.
This latter class is very widely extended, even
in the Semitic languages, as we have already
shown in the case of the root *lk* (see p. 84).
From the expression of disgust and fear, we get
awe, ugly, ἀγάομαι, ἀγάζομαι and their cognates;
from shuddering, the roots of φρίσσω, bristle,
hérisser, &c.; from the first sounds of infancy, we
get babe, *bambino*, babble, and many more; from

sounds of anger, "huff," and others; lastly, from "prut," a sound of arrogance, we get the word "proud," "pride," as in German, "trotzig," haughty, from "trotz,"* an interjection of defiance and contempt.

The other class of onomatopœias is far more extensive, and embraces the widest possible range of inanimate sounds. They may be ranged under the following heads; and although the examples are all taken from the †English language, they might be paralleled in almost any other.

1. Animal sounds, as quack, cackle, roar, neigh, whinny, bellow, mew, pur, croak, caw, chatter, bark, yelp, &c.

2. Inarticulate human sounds, as laugh, cough, sob, sigh, moan, shriek, yawn, whoop, weep, &c.

3. Collision of hard bodies, represented by p, t, k; as clap, rap, tap, flap, slap, rat-tat, &c.

4. Collision of softer bodies, represented by b, d, g; as dab, dub, bob, thud, dub-a-dub, &c.

---

* "Trotz alle dem," is Freiligrath's rendering of Burns' "for a' that." I may remark here, that many of these instances are borrowed from Mr. Wedgwood's *Etymol. Dictionary*, of which the first part only is yet printed. This work, although not free from errors, has the merit of having put forward some very clear and original views on this subject.

† Abridged from Mr. Wedgwood in the *Phil. Transac.* ii. 118.

5. Motion through the air, represented by z, &c.; as whizz, buzz, sough, &c.

6. Resonance, represented by m, n, &c.; as clang, knell, ring, twang, clang, din, &c.

7. Motion of liquids, &c., represented by sibilants, as clash, splash, plash, dash, swash, &c.

These are but specimens of the wide extent of these words in a language by no means the most remarkable for its adoption of onomatopœia. There are even broad general laws by which the various degrees of intensity in sound are expressed by the modification of vowels. Thus, high notes are represented by i, low broad sounds by a, and the change of a or o to i has the effect of diminution, as we see by comparing the words clap, clip, clank, clink, pock, peck, cat, kitten, foal, filly, tramp, trip, nob, nipple, &c. Another way of diminishing intensity is to soften a final letter, as in tug, tow, drag, draw, swagger, sway, stagger, stay, &c. Reduplication of syllables is a mode of expressing continuance, as in murmur, &c., and this effect is also produced by the addition of r and l, as in grab, grapple, wrest, wrestle, crack, crackle, dab, dabble, &c.

It is easy to see from the above examples that the onomatopœia and the interjection are the points from which language has developed itself, and from which "two separate lines of concurrent and * simultaneous evolution have proceeded." The manner in which the various parts of speech grew out of these elements, and which of them may be supposed to be logically or actually anterior to the rest, is a wide and difficult subject of inquiry on which much uncertainty must necessarily prevail, and with which we are hero unconcerned.

There is no doubt that, for some reason or other, many of our English onomatopœians are regarded as in some degree beneath the dignity of words, and are supposed to partake of the nature of vulgarity.† Yet with great inconsistency the places in which poets have been most successful in producing "an echo of the sound to the sense" are generally regarded with especial favour. The classic poets used this ornament with the most fastidious good taste. Even the ancients had learned to admire the rhyming

* Latham *on the Engl. Lang.* 4th ed. p. xlix. Heyse, *System*, s. 73 fg.

† Traces of this feeling are found in Quinctilian (*Instt. Orr.* i. 5). "Sed minime nobis concessa est ὀνοματοποιία. ... Jamne hinnire et balare fortiter diceremus, nisi judicio vetustatis niterentur ?" See, too, viji. 6. Other passages quoted by Lersch (*Sprachphilosophie*, i. s. 130), are Varro (*L. L.* v. p. 69) ; Diomed. iii. p. 453, &c. Plato calls it ἀπείκασμα, and the Grammarians ἀπὸ ἤχους.

termination by which Homer faintly recalls the
humming of the summer swarms, in the lines—

'Ήύτε ἔθνεα πολλὰ μελισσάων ἀδινάων
πέτρης ἐκ γλαφύρης ἀεὶ νέον ἐρχομενάων :

and yet they do not surpass the exquisite verses
of a living poet :—

> Myriads of rivulets hurrying through the lawn ;
> The moan of doves in immemorial elms,
> And murmur of innumerable bees.

Again, what can be more vivid than the marvellous way in which Homer recalls the snapping of
a shattered sword, in—

Τριχθί τε καὶ τετραχθὶ διατρύφεν :

which is incomparably superior to the much-
admired hemistich of Racine, "L'essieu crie et
se rompt." Both Homer and Virgil have imitated the rapid clatter of horses' hoofs with equal
felicity :—

Πολλὰ δ' ἄναντα, κάταντα, πάραντά τε δόχμιά τ' ἦλθον :
Quadrupedante putrem sonitu quatit ungula campum :

and the verse * in which Dubartas endeavours to

* " La gentile alouette avec son tire lire,
    Tire l'ire aux fachez, et tire-lirant tire
    Vers la route du ciel : puis son vol vers ce lieu
    Vire, et désire dire à dieu Dieu, à dieu Dieu."
The verse seems to me too laboured and unnatural.

recal the manner in which the lark "shoots up and shrills in flickering gyres," has met with numberless admirers.

The greatest of our modern poets, Mr. Tennyson, has perhaps been more unsparing and more successful in his use of this figure than any of his predecessors, and a few passages will show that onomatopœia judiciously used is capable of the noblest application. Take, for instance, the leap of a cataract, in—

> Where the river sloped
> To plunge in cataract, shattering on black blocks
> Its breadth of thunder;

or the shock of a *mêlée*, in—

> The storm
> Of galloping hoofs bare on the ridge of spears
> And riders front to front, until they closed
> In conflict with the crash of shivering points
> And thunder. . . .
> And all the plain—brand, mace, and shaft, and shield
> Shock'd, like an iron-clanging anvil banged
> With hammers;

or the booming of the sea, in—

> Roar rock-thwarted under bellowing.caves;

or, finally, what can be more perfect than the graphic power in which the picture of a fleet of glass wrecked on a reef of gold is called before us by the perfect adaptation of sound to sense, in the lines—

> For the fleet drew near,
> *Touched, clinked,* and *clashed,* and vanished.

Yet in all these cases we believe that it is to the language and not to the poet that the main credit is due. The language is the perfect instrument, and in the poet's hands it is used with perfect power; but were it not for the original perfection of his instrument he would be unable to produce such rich and varied results; he would be unable to place the picture before the eye by bringing into play that swift and subtle law of association whereby a reproduction of the sounds at once recalls to the inner eye the images or circumstances with which they are connected. In every case the consummate art and skill of the writer consists simply in choosing the proper words for the thought which he wishes to express, which words are always the simplest.   Appropriate * language is and always must be the most effective, and when a writer *clearly goes out of his*

---

* "Many at least of the celebrated passages that are cited as imitative in sound, were, on the one hand, not the result of accident, nor yet on the other hand of study ; but the idea (!) in the author's mind spontaneously suggested appropriate sounds."— Archbp. Whately's *Rhetoric,* iii. s. 2.

way to produce an effect he generally loses his effectiveness by abandoning simplicity. How much onomatopœia degenerates in a less skilful and artistic hand we might see in many instances, were not the selection of them an invidious task.

In short, an exquisite and instinctive taste can only decide on the extent to which this figure may be *consciously* used. We feel that Virgil was right in rejecting Ennius's

At tuba terribili sonitu taratantara dicit,

as the imitation of a trumpet-blast; and none but a comic poet (like Swift) would use rub-a-dub, dub-a-dub in English to express the beating of a drum: and yet who was ever otherwise than delighted with the word τήνελλα, in which Archilochus imitated the twang of a harp-string, and which the Greeks used ever afterwards as an expression of joyous triumph? Again, none but a comedian could have ventured on so direct an imitation of sounds as βρεκεκεκέξ κοάξ κοάξ, and yet no one could object to the pretty line in which Ovid tries to produce the same impression :—

Quamquam sunt sub aquâ, sub aquâ maledicere tentant.

The misuse of language fails to produce the echo which its simple and natural use would not have failed to awake. In short, it is in many cases impossible to use language which shall be at once specific and appropriate without being forced to adopt imitative words. There is no style required in order to speak of the booming of the cannon, the twang of the bowstring, the hurtling of the arrow, the tolling or pealing of the bell, the rolling or throbbing of the drum, the sough or whisper of the breeze, because in each case the proper word is ready for us at once in the language which we speak, and if we are to speak naturally we can use no other. The harmonies of language arise mainly from this power of imitation, and a sensuous language is always energetic, poetic, passionate.

CHAPTER V.

THE DEVELOPMENT OF ROOTS.

Language is like the minim immortal among the infusoria, which keeps splitting itself into halves.—COLERIDGE.

THE most brilliant of modern philosophers, M. Victor Cousin, in endeavouring to refute the conclusion of Locke that all words draw their first origin from sensible ideas, adduces the pronoun " I " and the verb " to be " as words which are primitive, indecomposible, and irreducible in every language with which he is acquainted—as words which are pure signs, representing nothing whatever except the meaning conventionally attached to them, and having no connection with sensible ideas.

Whatever may become of M. Cousin's general proposition, the instances which he has chosen to support it are very unfortunate, for it may be clearly proved that these words, abstract as they may appear, are yet derived from sensible images. An examination of them will therefore help us to gain a little insight into the origin of language,

H

and perhaps strengthen our suspicion that even
the most subjective words, which merely intimate
intellectual relations, even the words which express the essential categories, may be ultimately
proved to have a metaphorical and not a psychological origin. Such a conviction will by no
means impair the dignity of language, or cast a
slur on the majesty of thought; for if the entire
lexicon of every language be capable of being
reduced to a number of sensational roots, the no
less important element of Grammar always remains as the indisputable result of the pure
reason. And not only so, but even the possibility of accepting imitative roots as *signs* of the
thing imitated, supposes (as M. Maine * de Biran
acutely observes) the pre-existence of an activity
superior to sensation, whereby the thinking
being places himself outside the circle of impressions and images in order to signify and note
them.

It might be supposed that the word by which
a man characterises himself in relation to his
own consciousness would be of a very mysterious

* *Essai sur les fondements de psychologie.* The same psycho-
logist in his Essay on the Origin of Language says of those who
maintain a revealed language, that they give us " comme article
de foi une hypothèse arbitraire et amphibologique."—*Œuvres
Inéd.de Maine de Biran*, iii. pp. 229—278.

and abstract character, because it must express the notion of individuality, which might be regarded as a very primary intuition. This, however, is far from being the case. Man regarded himself as an object before he learnt to regard himself as a subject, and hence " the objective cases of the personal as well as of the other pronouns are always older than the subjective," and the Sanskrit *mâm, ma* (Greek με, Latin *me*) is earlier than *aham* (ἐγών, and *ego*). We might have conjectured this from the fact already noticed, that children learn to speak of themselves in the third person, *i. e.* regard themselves as objects long before they acquire the power of representing their material selves as the instrument of an abstract entity. A child* does not attain to the free use of the pronoun "I" until the acquisition of formal grammar outstrips the psychological growth. And the same takes place with other personal pronouns. Man's primary consciousness of his own existence is nearly simultaneous with the belief that he is something separate from the not-me, the external world. But at first he would only regard this external world as an immense inseparable phe-

* See some admirable remarks to this effect in Mr. F. Whalley Harper's excellent book on the *Power of Greek Tenses.*

nomenon, and it would be some time before he
could "invest the * not-me with the powers of
agency and will which we experience in ourselves."

But whether the conception of individuality be
regarded as coming early or late, so far is the
pronoun " I " from involving any sublime intrinsic
meaning, that it was originally a demonstrative
monosyllable, indicative of a particular position.
"In fact," says Dr. Donaldson, "the primitive
pronouns must have been very simple words, for
the first and easiest articulations would naturally
be adopted to express the primary intuition of
space.   These little vocables denote only the
immediate relations of locality.   It is reasonable
to suppose that the primitive pronouns would be
designations of *here* and *there*, of the subject and
object as contrasted and opposed to one another.
As soon as language becomes a medium of communication between two speaking persons, a
threefold distinction at once arises between the
here or subject, the *there* or object, and the person spoken to or considered as a subject in himself, though an object in regard to the speaker."
In other words, there are " three † primitive rela-

* Donaldson's *New Cratylus*, p. 220, 4th ed.
† Donaldson's *Greek Grammar*, s. 67—79.

tions of position : here, near to here, and there,
or juxtaposition, proximity, and distance. The
three primitive articulations which are used (in
Greek) to express these three relations of position, are the three primitive *tenues*, Π, Ϙ, T,
pronounced pa, qua, ta, which we shall call the
first, second, and third pronominal elements.
The first pronominal element denoting juxtaposition, or *here*, is used to express (a) the first
personal pronoun ; (b) the first numeral ; (c) the
point of departure in motion. The second pronominal element denoting proximity, or *near to
the here*, is used to express (a) the second personal pronoun ; (b) the relative pronoun ; (c) the
reflexive pronoun. The third pronominal element, denoting distance, is used to express (a) the
third personal pronoun ; (b) negation ; (c) separation." * Thus, then, we find that even so metaphysical a conception as that of individuality is
only expressed by an elementary word implying
locality.

We see, therefore, that M. Cousin is mistaken
in supposing that the pronouns at any .rate
were non-sensational in their origin, arising as
they do from the very earliest and simplest of all

* For the development and more clear enunciation of these
views, we must refer to the works quoted.

sensations. And it is, perhaps, still more surprising to find that a similar origin can be traced even
in the numerals, which involved the very triumph
of abstraction ; for, in using a numeral, " we strip
things of all their sensible properties,* and consider them as merely relations of number, as
members of a series, as perfectly general relations of place." And yet abstract as they are,
and, absolutely as we might suppose them to be
removed from concrete objects of sense, it is a
matter of certainty that their genesis can be traced.
About the general result few philologists have
any doubt, however much they may differ in their
details. "I do† not think," says M. Bopp,
*" that any language whatever has produced special
original words for the particular designation of
such compacted and peculiar ideas as three, four,
five, &c."* Accordingly it has been proved that
the three first numerals in Sanskrit and Greek
are connected with the three personal pronouns,
and originally implied here,‡ near to the here, and

---

* Donaldson's *New Crat.* ch. ii. Plato (*Crat.* p. 435) thought
the numerals offered a proof that at least *some* part of language
must be the result of convention and custom (συνθήκη καὶ ἔθος).

† Bopp's *Comparative Grammar*, § 311.

‡ Dr. Donaldson aptly compares (*New Crat.* § 154) the vulgarism
"number one" as a synonym for the first person, and " proximus
sum egomet mihi."

there; that the *fourth** implies 1 + 3; that the
fifth, as might have been expected, is connected
with the same root as the word "hand;" that
the tenth numeral means two hands, and so
forth.

Still it might be supposed that the verb
"to be," predicating as it does the quality of
existence, a conception so abstract that the profoundest metaphysicians and physiologists have
been as yet wholly unable to find for it any
tolerable definition, would resist all attempts at
a reduction to any sensational root. If we are to
look to a definition of "life" as being either un-
discoverable, or else a discovery which can only be
expected from the ultimate triumphs of science,
surely we might suppose that here at least it is
impossible to find a sensible idea as the root of
the sublime verbs which are the means of repre-

---

* Bopp's *Comparative Grammar,* §§ 309, 323. Donaldson's
New Crat. ch. ii. ; *Greek Gram.* § 240. For the Hebrew numerals
see *Maskil-le Sophir.* pp. 41 sq., by the same author. Other
works are Pott, *Die quinäre und vigesimale Zählmethode.*
Halle, 1847. Mommsen, in Höfer's *Zeitschr. für die Wiss. der
Spr.* Heft. 2, 1846. In Greenland the word for 20 is "a man,"
(i.e. fingers + toes = 20); and for 100 the word is *five men,* &c.
It might have been thought that particles were eminently (wb
Aristotle calls them) φωναὶ ἄσημοι, and yet even *their* pedig
may be traced ; and in fact no clear line of distinction can
drawn between them and the φωναὶ σημαντικαί.—Heyse, s. 108;

senting life as an attribute.   But we are all liable
to the error of forming far too * high an estimate
of the intrinsic vitality (the supposed *occulta vis*)
of verbs in general.   They contain no inherent
powers which separate them from nouns, and
their supposed distinctive character arises entirely out of their combination with a subject.
The fancy (for instance) that "the root *can* 'sing'
differs from *can* 'song' in the same degree that
a magnetised steel bar differs from an ordinary
one, or a charged Leyden jar from a discharged
one," is proved by minute analysis to be totally
groundless.   And the importance of the verb
"to be" in particular has been greatly exagge-
rated, as though it were a necessary ingredient
of every logical proposition.   For in many languages the verb is wanting altogether, and its
mere *implication* is quite sufficient for all logical
purposes.   "The verb-substantive," observes
Mr. Garnett (from whose most valuable Essay on
the nature and analysis of the verb we have

* For instance, we find M. A. Vinet (*Essais de Philos. Morale*,
p. 323) speaking of the verb as the word which founds, or, so
to speak, creates an ideal world side by side with the real world,
and of which the real world is either the expression or the type.
The word "verb" has often been dwelt on as showing the importance attached to this part of speech; the German "*zeitwort*"
is more to the purpose.   The Chinese call it *ho-tseu*, or the living
word (Silvestre de Sacy, *Principes de Gram. Gén.* i. ch. 1.)

borrowed these suggestions), " if considered as necessary to vivify all connected speech and bind together the terms of every logical proposition, is much upon a footing with the phlogiston of the chemists of the last generation, regarded as a necessary pabulum of combustion—that is to say, *Vox et præterea nihil.*"

Whatever our *à priori* estimate of the power of the verb-substantive may be, its origin is traced by philology to very humble and material sources. The Hebrew verbs הָוָה (houa), or הָיָה (haia), may very probably be derived from an onomatopœia of respiration. The verb *kama*, which has the same sense, means primitively " to stand out," and the verb *koum*,* to stand, passes into the sense of " being." In Sanskrit, *as-mi* (from which all the verbs-substantive in the Indo-European languages are derived, as εἰμί, *sum*, am; Zend, *ahmi;* Lithuanic, *esmi;* Icelandic, *em,* &c.), is, properly speaking, no verbal root, but " a formation on the demonstrative pronoun *sa*, the idea meant to be conveyed being simply that of local presence." And of the two other

---

* Compare the Italian *stare*, Spanish *estar*. Prof. Key (*Trans. of Phil. Soc.* vol. iv.) quotes an anecdote of a lady who had to tell her African servant, "Go and fetch big teacup, he *live* in pantry." We cannot, however, accept his derivations of "case" from "edo," and "vivo" from "bibo."

roots used for the same purpose, viz. *bhu* (φύω, *fui*, &c.), and *sthá* (*stare*, &c.),* the first is probably an imitation of breathing, and the second notoriously a physical verb, meaning "to stand up." May we not, then, ask with Bunsen, "What is '*to be*' in all languages but the spiritualisation of *walking* or *standing* or *eating* ? "

Perhaps if we were to try to think of any *positive* word which it would be *impossible* to derive from a root imitative of sound, it would be the word *silence*. And yet we believe that the root of even this word is a simple onomatopœia, and that it is connected with the sibilants (hush! whish ! &c.), by which we endeavour to call attention to the fact that we desire to listen intently. It may help us to accept this etymology

---

* See Renan, p. 129. Becker, *Organism der Sprache*, p. 58. In point of fact, the conception of existence in untaught minds is generally concrete, and often grossly material. Vico mentions the fact, that peasants often say of a sick person "he still eats," for "he still lives." "In the Lingua Franca the more abstract verbs have disappeared altogether; 'to be' is always expressed by 'to stand,' and 'to have' by 'to hold.'

' Non *tener* honta
Questo *star* la ultima affronta.'

This shows the tendency of language to degradation when not upheld by literary culture and elevated thought. Barbarism proved as efficacious in materialising the conception of the Latin races, as in sweeping away the niceties of their grammar. To this day the Spaniards say, *tengo hambre*, for *esurio*."—R. G.

if we observe that the colloquialism "to be *mum*" undoubtedly arises* from an imitation of the sound by which we express the closing of the lips.

If we fully allow that a considerable number of roots *have* (and *must* have) sprung from the instinctive principle which we have been endeavouring to illustrate, we have gone very far to show what was the origin of language. For the permutations and combinations of which a very few roots† are capable, and the rich variety of applications of which each separate root admits, are almost inconceivable to any who have not, by a study of the subject, rendered themselves familiar with the processes of the human mind. Indeed, a superfluity of roots argues a feebleness of conception, and a superabundant vocabulary is an impediment to thought.   In the Society Isles they have one word for the tail of a dog, another for the tail of a bird, and a third for the tail of a sheep, and yet for "tail" itself,‡—" tail " in the

---

* See Wedgwood, p. xvii.

† Who would have thought à *priori* that the word "stranger" has its root in the single vowel *e*, the Latin preposition for "from" ?   Yet we see it to be so, "the moment that the intermediate links of the chain are submitted to our examination,— e, ex, extra, extraneus, étranger, stranger."—Dugald Stewart, *Philos. Es.* p. 217, 4th ed.

‡ Adelung, *Mithridates*, iii. 6, p. 325.

abstract, they have no word whatever. Again, the Mohicans have words for wood-cutting, cutting the head, the arm, &c., and yet no verb meaning simply to cut. But all the specific words are comparatively of very little use; in point of fact they are encumbrances, rather than treasures. It is the sign of an advancing language to modify or throw away these superfluities of special terms. Thus the number of roots decreases continually; in Sanskrit, there are* 2,000; in Gothic, not more than 600; while 250 are said to be sufficient to supply the modern German with its 80,000 words.

The processes by which this retrenchment is carried on are the derivation, and composition of necessary and existing uses to supersede the continual invention of new ones. The laws by which these processes are effected are for the most part regular and universal, and the discovery of them constitutes the great reward of modern philology. But as our present inquiries are only of the most general and preliminary nature, we must confine ourselves here to giving one or two short and comparatively easy specimens of what we may term the elasticity or diffusiveness of roots.

We have already alluded to the root " ach," as

* Benloew, *De la Science Comp. des Langues*, p. 22.

having been in all probability an onomatopœian which gives rise to a large number of cognate words in the Indo-European languages. It is at any rate interesting to observe how this root, however originated, suffices to express alike material sharpness, bodily sensations, and mental emotions. M. Garnett* gives the following brief list of examples:—"Ἄκω, ἄκανθα, ἀχὶς, αἰχμῆ, acuo, acus, acies; Teutonic, ekke (edge), ackes (axe); Icelandic, eggia, to sharpen, to exhort, to egg on; German, ecke, a corner; Bavarian, igeln, prurire (German, jucken; Scotch, yeuk; English, itch) —acken (to ache), ἄχος (grief); Anglo-Saxon, ege, fear—egeslich, horrible; Icelandic, ecki, sorrow; German, ekel, disgust; with very many more. It is possible that Anglo-Saxon ege, an eye, may be of the same family. Compare the Latin phrase, acies oculorum."

Or, again, let us take the Sanskrit root dhu, to move about, to agitate. A list of the derivatives from this root in various Indo-European languages would fill several pages, but we will only supply one or two. First, then, we get the verbs θύω and θύνω, to rush, or move violently, with their derivatives, as θύελλα, a storm; θύννος, a thunny-fish (from its rapid, darting motion);

* Essay on English Dialects, p. 64.

θύσανος, a waving, fluttering tassel; θυιὰς, a bacchanal; θύρσος, the shaken thyrsus, or ivy-wreathed wand, the symbol of Bacchic frenzy; θορεῖν, to leap; θοῦρος, impetuous; ἀθύρω, to play; and among many others, θυμὸς, the mind, from the same property which struck the poet, in saying—

> How swift is the glance of the mind !
>   Compared with the speed of its flight
> E'en the tempest itself lags behind,
>   And the swift-speeding arrows of light !

From the same root we get θύω, to sacrifice, from the striking aspect of the rising and curling fumes, when the victim lay burning on the altar; θύμος, thyme, from the use made of that herb in fumigations; *fumus*, smoke; θυμέλη, the altar in the centre of the orchestra; and many more. Lastly, we may mention the curious word θοάζειν, which is used in the apparently contradictory senses of "to move hastily," and "to sit."

The curious phenomenon presented by the latter word, of the same root serving for two directly opposite meanings, is one worthy of the greatest attention; and we believe that it has

---

* Still more strange are the variations presented by the root ἕω. See Leibnitz, *Nouv. Ess. sur l'Entendement Humain*, iii. 2. 2; and Donaldson's *New Crat.* p. 476.

first been definitely noticed by modern philologists. "Contrast," says Archdeacon Hare, "is a kind of relation;" and the suggestion of contrarieties may even be regarded as a primary law of the association of ideas. It is this principle which accounts for the apparently strange fact that opposite conditions are expressed by the same root slightly modified. Thus, to select some of the instances collected by Dr. Donaldson,* our own word "dear" has the two meanings of "prized," because you have it, and "expensive," because you want it; and "fast" has the opposite senses of "fixed" and "rapid." Similarly, χρεία in Greek means both "use" and "need"; and λάω means both "to wish" and "to take;" while aio, αὐδάω, and καλέω, "I speak," or "call," are singularly like ἀΐω, audio, and κλύω, "I hear."†

---

* *New Crat.* p. 80.

† The "lucus à non lucendo" principle, which explained various positive words as though they were derived from the *absence* of the quality they attributed, has long been given up by all sound scholars. Of course such names as Euxinus, Beneventum, Εὐμενίδες, "good folk," "crétin," "natural," &c., arise in a totally different manner, as well as the name Parcæ, absurdly derived "a non parcendo." The supposed instances of "Antiphrasis," as the grammarians called it, are eminently absurd, e.g. Varro, *L. L.* iv. 8: "Cœlum, contrario nomine *celatum*, quod apertum est." Donat. *de Trop.* p. 1778: "Bellum, hoc est minimè

Another instance of the same peculiarity arises from the different objective or subjective relations which any phenomenon may present, some of which relations may be strongly contrasted; e. g., a " key " might derive its name either from opening or shutting. Thus, to adopt some of the cases mentioned by Mr. Garnett,* the numeral *one* gives rise to compounds of apparently opposite signification. From the Irish *aon*, " one," we have *aonach*, " a waste," and also " an assembly ;" *aontugadh*, celibacy, and *aontumadh*, marriage. The Latin *unicus* implies singularity, but *unitas* implies association. " The concord of this discord is easily found, if we consider that the term *one* may either refer to *one* as an *individual*, or in the sense of an *aggregate*." Similarly, it is not difficult to explain the apparent anomaly that σχόλη means both " school " and " leisure," and that " lee " has very different acceptations in lee-*side* and lee-*shore*. Other examples might easily be found, all tending to prove that " as rays of light may be reflected and refracted in all possible ways from their primary direction, so the meaning of a word may

bellum." They confused it with irony and euphemism. See Lersch, i. s. 132, 133.

* *Essays*, p. 234 sq.

be deflected from its original bearing in a variety of manners; and consequently we cannot well reach the primitive force of the term unless we know the precise gradations through which it has gone."

It has been proved, then, in this chapter, that a few onomatopœic roots would give a sufficient basis on which to rear the largest superstructure of language, and we have shown how in some cases an imitative origin may be discovered even in words which might have been expected to defy analysis. Into the methods adopted in this rich variety of applications we must inquire more closely in the following chapter, but we must here remark that, as it was by the association of ideas that even the most heterogeneous and contrary relations were expressed by the same root, so the words themselves tend powerfully to establish new points of association, and to facilitate the astonishing rapidity of thought. By the aid of verbal signs we exercise an enormous power over all our faculties, for in repeating the sign we are enabled by the personal activity of our will to recall the image which it represents, and submit that image to our control.* Our sensa-

* *Dict. des Sciences Philosoph.* p. 646. Locke *on the Under.* III. ii. 6.

tions, transformed into thought, come and go at our bidding, and we extend and multiply them without limit.

Awake but one, and lo, what myriads rise !

By virtue of an active imagination the fathers of the human race produced the mighty heritage of speech, and made the utterance of their lips a means of recalling their sensations and expressing their thoughts ; in *consequence* of the activity of the imagination, our words become the tyrants of our convictions, and our phrases " often repeated, ossify the very organs of intelligence."

Hence the blood of nations has often ere now been shed from an inability to see the synthesis of various truths in some single threadbare shibboleth of party ; and a mistaken theory embalmed in a * widely-received word has re-

---

* Thus the long opposition to the Newtonian theory in France rose mainly from the influence of the word "attraction." See Comte's *Pos. Philos.* (Martineau's ed.) i. p. 182. For the tremendous consequences of the introduction of the term "*landed proprietor*" into Bengal, see Mill's *Logic*, ii. 232. It caused "a disorganisation of society which had not been introduced into that country by the most ruthless of its barbarian invaders." "Fetish," as adopted by the negroes from the Portuguese, "feiticão" (sorcery), is an instance of a word changing meaning with the feeling of the speakers.

tarded for centuries the progress of knowledge.
For, as Bacon wisely says, "Men believe that
their reason is lord over their words, but it
happens, too, that words exercise a reciprocal
and reactionary power over the intellect," and
that "words, as a Tartar's bow, do shoot back
upon the understanding of the wisest, and
mightily entangle and pervert the judgment."

There is one moral application of the truths
we have been considering, which we should do
well not to omit; it is the far-reaching danger
of idle * or careless words ; it is the solemn
admonition—

Guard well thy thoughts, for thoughts are heard in Heaven!

---

* ἤθους χαρακτήρ ἐστι τ' ἀνθρώπου λόγος.—Stob. The language
of a people expresses its genius and its character.—Bacon, *De
Augm. Scient.* vi. i. Cf. Diog. Laert. p. 58. Quinct. xi. p. 675.
Cic. *Tusc. Disp.* v. 16.

CHAPTER VI.

METAPHOR.

" Die Sinnlichkeit erzeugt, auf der ersten stufe der Wortschöp-
fung, ein *Abbild;* die Einbildungskraft, auf der zweiten, ein *Symbol;*
der Verstand, endlich, auf der dritten, ein *Zeichen* für das object."
—HEYSE, *System der Sprachwissenschaft, s.* 95.

" Every language is a dictionary of faded metaphors."—RICHTER.

IF it be impossible for us to *know* any single
particle of matter in itself; if we are unable to
do more than express the *relations* of any single
external phenomenon; how can we hope to give
an accurate nomenclature to the *noumena,* the
inward emotions, the immaterial conceptions, the
abstract entities which we cannot touch or handle,
and which have an existence only for the intellect and the heart ? How can we make the
modulations of the voice the symbols * for the
passions of the soul ?

In mathematics there is a line, known as the
asymptote, which continually approaches to a
curve, but, being produced for ever, does not cut

* Ἔστι μὲν οὖν τὰ ἐν τῇ φωνῇ τῶν ἐν τῇ ψυχῇ παθημάτων
σύμβολα—Arist. *De Interp.* L i.

it, though the distance between the asymptote
and the curve becomes, in the course of this
approach, less than any assignable quantity.
Language, in relation to thought, must ever be
regarded as an *asymptote*. They can no more
perfectly coincide than any two particles of matter
can be made absolutely to touch each other.
No power of language enables man to reveal the
features of the mystic Isis, on whose statue was
inscribed : " I am all which hath been, which is,
and shall be, and no mortal hath ever lifted my
veil." Now, as ever, a curtain of shadow must
hang between—

> That hidden life, and what we see and hear.

No single virtue, no single faculty, no single
spiritual truth, no single metaphysical conception, can be expressed without the aid of analogy
or metaphor. Metaphor—the transference of a
word from its usual meaning to an analogous
one—is the intellectual agent of language, just
as onomatopœia is the mechanical agent. Metaphor and catachresis (*i. e.*, the use of the same
word to express two different things which are
supposed to present some analogy to each other,
as when "sweet" is applied to sounds) have
been called the two channels of expression

which irrigate the wide field of human intelligence. By their means language, though poor
in vocables, was rich in thought, and resembled
in its power the one coin* of the Wandering
Jew, which always sufficed for all his needs,
and always took the impress of the sovereign
regnant in the countries through which he
passed.

We might have easily conjectured that such
would be the case. "Man, by the action of all his
faculties, is carried out of himself and towards
the exterior world; the phenomena of the exterior world are those which strike him first, and
those, therefore, are the ones which receive the
first names, which names are, so to speak, tinted
with the colours of the objects they express. But,
afterwards, when man turns his attention inwards,
he sees distinctly those intellectual phenomena,
of which he had previously had only a confused
perception, and when he wishes to express those
new phenomena of the soul and of thought,
analogy leads him to apply the signs which he is
looking for to the signs which he already possesses; for analogy is the law of every nascent
or developed language; hence come the metaphors into which analysis resolves the ma-

* Nodier, p. 65.

jority of the signs for the most abstract moral ideas." [*]

To call things which we have never seen before by the name of that which appears to us most nearly to resemble them, is a practice of every-day life. That children at first call all men " father," and all women " mother," is an observation as old as Aristotle.[†] The Romans gave the name of Lucanian *ox* to the elephant, and *camelopardus* to the giraffe, just as the New Zealanders are stated to have called " horses " large *dogs*. The astonished Caffirs gave the name of *cloud* to the first parasol which they had seen ; and similar instances might be adduced almost indefinitely. They prove that it is an instinct, if it be not a necessity to borrow for the unknown the names already used for things known.

But although we can absolutely trace this process in so many cases, that we are entitled to *infer*, with Locke, that *every* word expressing facts which do not fall under the senses, is yet ultimately derived from sensible ideas, we cannot

---

[*] Victor Cousin, *Cours de Phil.* iii. Leçon Vingtième.

[†] Φύσικα, i. 1. The name alligator (Spanish, *el lagarto*, *the* lizard) is another instance of the same kind of thing, as indeed is the Greek κροκόδειλος.

expect to *prove* this in every particular instance. When a standard of value is once introduced among nations, it is almost always a coinage of the precious metals; but when public credit is firmly established, a paper currency is allowed freely to circulate. And so in language many terms have become purely arbitrary, and in themselves valueless, which now pass unquestioned in their conventional meaning, but have lost all traces of the process to which they owed their origin, and retain no longer, the impress of the thought which they originally conveyed.

Illustrations are not far to seek; indeed, we can hardly utter a sentence which will not supply them, of which the very word "illustration" is itself an instance. Thus, in Hebrew, the words for "anger" and "the nose" are identical,* and even in Greek, πρᾶος τὴν ῥίνα, "gentle in nose," is used for "of gentle disposition." Every reader of the Bible will recognise that "a melting of the heart" is the metaphor for despair; a "loosening of the reins" for fear; a "high carriage of the head" for pride; "stiffness of

---

* See Renan, 120 sqq. Theocrit. ii. 18. The French word colère is from χόλος, bile; our word anger, from the root "ang" ἄγχι, ἀγχονή, angle, angina, angustus, &c.) implying compression. The Greek στόμαχος explains itself.

neck " for obstinacy; " thirst" or "pallor " for
fear; a " turning of the face " for favour. It is
this word·painting, this eagerness * for graphic
touches, that gives to Hebrew its vivid, picturesque, impetuous character. It is interesting
to observe how necessary to them it became.
Even when they have by long usage learnt to
accept a special word as the sign of some moral
sentiment or mental emotion, they love to add to
it *also* a picture of the physical circumstance.
This is the explanation of such apparent pleo-
nasms, as " he opened his mouth and said,"
" he answered and said," " he was angry and his
visage fell," " he was angry and his visage was
enflamed." It is the result of that vital energy
which enkindled the soul of prophets and poets ;
which exalted the intellect of a nation, fully
conscious that it had a mighty mission to per-
form. Spontaneous imagery is the characteristic
of all passionate thought.

The Hebrews were not the only nation which
sought for open and confessed metaphors in their
style, when the bright colours of the original
picture-word had grown too dim to recall the

* πρὸ ὀμμάτων ποιεῖν. For abundant instances of Hebrew
metaphors see Glasaii *Philologia Sacra*, where there is a long
chapter on the subject.

image which they once presented. We feel instinctively that certain states of mind can only be described by a comparison with the natural appearance which offers the nearest analogy to them. " A lamb is innocence ; a snake is subtle spite. Flowers express to us the delicate affections. Light and darkness are our familiar expressions for knowledge and ignorance. Visible distance behind and before us is respectively our image of memory and of hope." *

Again, to take the first group of English words which present themselves, what is " imagination" or "reflection" but the summoning up of a picture before the inward eye? What is " comprehension " but a grasping ; "disgust" but an unpleasant taste ; "insinuation" but a getting into the bosom of anything? Courage is "good heart ; " "rectitude" a perpendicular position; "austerity" is dryness ; " superciliousness " a raising of the eyebrow ; "humility" is something cognate to the ground ; "fortune" is the falling of a lot ; "*virtue*" is that which becomes a *man;* "humanity" is the proper characteristic of our race ; "courtesy" is borrowed from palaces ; "calamity" is the hurrying of the wind among the reeds. What are "aversion"† and " inclination" but a

* Emerson's *Nature.*   † Compare ἐφίεμαι, ὀρέγομαι.

turning away from, and a bending towards ?
"Error " is a wandering out of the way; "envy"
is looking upon another with an evil eye; an
"emotion " is a movement of the soul; " influence" recalls the ripple circling on the surface
of a stream; " heaven " is the canopy *heaved* over
our heads ; " hell " is the *hollow* space beneath our
feet; "religion " is a solemn study, or a binding,
or a new * choice; an " angel " is a messenger;
the "spirit" is but a breath of air.

The last etymology reminds us that we can
carry our proofs of what we assert into still
higher regions, even the transcendental regions
of human faith and worship. " Mystery" is
derived from " mu," the imitation of closing the
lips ; " priest" from " presbuteros," elder ; "sacrament" is deduced from the meaning " oath;"
"baptism " is dipping; " propitiation " is bringing near; " wisdom " is that which we have seen;
even the word for God himself, in Sanskrit as
in Chinese, means but the bright ether† or
starry sky.

* Three derivations have been proposed: *re-lego*, Cio. *de Nat.
Deor.* ii. 23; *re-ligo*, Lact. *Div. Inst.* 4; *re-eligo*, Augustin,
de Civ. Dei, x. 3. See Fleming's *Vocabulary of Philosophy*.

† See Bunsen's *Outlines*, ii. 142 seqq. Dyaus, θεὸς, deus, &c.,
from the root *div*, to shine. The derivation of our English word
"God" is doubtful; but I fear the beautiful belief that it is

To illustrate this necessity of metaphor any farther would be superfluous, since the materials for doing so are sufficiently abundant for any student who wishes to pursue the subject. The philosophical examination of the thoughts which are thus involved in concrete images is a most valuable inquiry, and one which opens a field of inexhaustible interest. The metaphors which we are thus forced to adopt are a living memorial* of the quick perceptions, the poetic intuitions, the deep insight of our ancestors: or are else a perpetuation of their unaccountable caprices of feeling or fancy, their vulgar errors and groundless suppositions. It sometimes happens that

deduced from "good" must be abandoned. Grimm (*Deutsch Myth.* p. 12) shows that there is a grammatical difference between the words in the Teutonic language signifying "God" and "good;" *if* the Persian "Khoda" can be derived from the Zend "qvadâta," Sanskrit "svadata," *à se datus, increatus,* a very appropriate etymology would be given.

* See Dugald Stewart's *Philosoph. Essays,* p. 217, 4th ed. Compare the widely different conceptions of happiness involved in the derivations of two such words as "beatus" and "selig." Or take the word "poet;" if in these days of wider knowledge and shallower thought, we find it nearly impossible to frame a satisfactory definition of poetry, how should we have been able to invent the word itself, which goes to the very root of the matter, by at once attributing to "the maker" that divine creative faculty whereby he is enabled "to give airy nothing a local habitation and a name!"

in all languages, the same analogy has been thus seized upon for a transitive "application," as in the words רוּחַ, πνεῦμα, anima, spirit, which all mean 'wind;' but, more frequently, different aspects of the same phenomenon have led to a different nomenclature; thus, "to think" is in Hebrew "to *speak;*" and among the savages of the Pacific it is "to speak in the stomach;" while in French it means "to weigh," and in Greek it is often described by a word borrowed from the deep purpling* of an agitated sea.

We call an expression metaphoric when it is applied in such a way that we glide lightly over its primary and obvious meaning to attach to it one which is secondary and more indirect. We call an expression a *catachresis* when it is used inappropriately, although custom may have sanctioned the use of it in the inappropriate sense; *e. g.*, when we speak of "an arm of the sea," the word "arm" is a catachresis; and when Shakspeare uses the phrase "To take up arms against a sea of troubles," it is only the use of this figure twice in the same line that forces on us a sense of incongruity.

Catachresis, as well as metaphor, has given rise to a large set of terms, phrases, and expressions;

* χαλκαίνω, πορφύρω.

and it is in one sense bolder than metaphor, because it takes words without any modification to
apply them to fresh emergencies. Thus, very
often words applicable to one sense are adopted
to express the sensations of another. That there
is * an analogy between the manners in which
they are affected no one will deny. The plant
" heliotrope " recalls by its smell the taste which
has given it its vulgar name; the king of
Hanover knew from the overture to a piece of
music, that the scene of it was supposed to be
a wood ; Saunderson, who was born blind, compared the colour *red* to the blowing of a trumpet,
or the crowing of a cock. There is, therefore,
no inherent absurdity, though there is much
affectation, in such lines as Ford's—

> What's that I *saw !* a sound !

and Donne's—

> A loud perfume ;

and Herbert's—

> His beams shall help my song, and both so twine,
> Till e'en his beams sing and my music shine.

It is against catachresis rather than against
metaphor that philosophers should have in-

* "Une lumière éclate, des couleurs crient, des idées se
heurtent, la mémoire bronche, le cœur murmure, l'obstination se
cadre contre les difficultés."—Nodier, p. 45.

veighed. "There is," says Seneca, "a vast number of things without names, which we call, not by proper designations, but by borrowed and adapted ones. We apply the word 'foot,' both to our own foot and that of a couch, and of a sail, and of a page, though these things are naturally distinct. But this results from the poverty of language." "It is a ridiculous sterility," says Voltaire, "to have been ignorant how to express otherwise an *arm* of the sea, an *arm* of a balance, an *arm* of a chair; it is a poverty of intellect which leads us to speak equally of the *head* of a nail, and the *head* of an army." It is this very frequent use of homonyms which leads to such great uncertainty about the meaning of many Hebrew words. Catachresis ought to be sparingly applied, and it possesses none of the advantages which arise from metaphor.

When the Megarians wanted assistance from the Spartans, they threw down an empty meal-bag before the assembly, and declared that "it lacked meal." The Laconic criticism "that the mention of the sack was superfluous," cannot be considered a fair one, because the action gave far more point to the request. When the Scythian ambassadors wished to prove to Darius the hopelessness of invading their country, instead of

making a long harangue, they argued with infinitely more force by merely bringing him a bird,
a mouse, a frog, and two arrows, to imply, that
unless he could soar like a bird, burrow like a
mouse, and hide in the marshes like a frog, he
would never be able to escape their shafts. The
tall poppyheads that Tarquinius lopped off with
his stick in the presence of the messenger of
Sextus, conveyed more vividly the intended lesson
than any amount of diabolical advice; and
turning* to Jewish history, we shall find that
the prophets found it necessary to illustrate
even *their* language (metaphorical as it was) by
living pictures—the rending of a garment, the
hiding of a girdle, the pushing with iron horns
—in order to bring home a vivid sense of conviction to the gross hearts of the people whom
they taught.

But when such outward illustrations are impossible, we adopt a shadow of them by painting with
words. When we speak of the cornfields standing so thick with corn, that they laugh and sing;
when we speak of the harvests thirsting, or of the
green fields sleeping in the quiet sunshine; when
we speak of the thunderbolts of eloquence, or the

* For the facts alluded to in this passage, see Herod. iii. 46,
iv. 132.   Liv. i. 54.   Jerem. xix. 10, &c.

dewy close of tender music, our language is
understood perhaps with more rapidity, and
our meaning expressed with greater clearness,
than if we were to translate the same phrases
into more prosaic and less imaginative expression.

Even the unimaginative *Aristotle observed
the fact. Mere names, he says, carry to the
mind of the hearer their specific meaning, and
there they end; but metaphors do more than
this, for they awaken new thoughts. Let us take
Aristotle's own example of the word " age," and
instead of Solomon's fine expression, "when the
almond-tree shall flourish, and the grasshopper
be a burden," substitute "when the hair is
white, and the body decrepit;" who does not
see that the force and poetry of the passage is
evaporated at once?

And, in point of fact, we do not go at all nearer
to truth by a substitution of terms that imply no
direct figure. Eloquence, for instance, has in
all ages been compared to thunder† and lightning,
because the effect of it upon the mind is closely
analogous to that produced by the bursting of a

* Arist. *Rhet.* iii. 10.
† ἤστραπτ', ἐβρόντα, κἀνεκύκα τὴν Ἑλλάδα.—Aristoph. "Proinde
tona eloquio."—Virg. *Æn.* xi.

storm; and when, out of dislike to such expressions, we talk of eloquence as having been passionate, or forcible, or effective, the impressions we convey are not nearly so powerful, or nearly so descriptive. And in many cases we must rest content to leave our emotions unexpressed, if we will not condescend to use the assistance of figurative terms. "Language," says Mr. Carlyle, "is the flesh-garment of Thought. I said that Imagination wove this flesh-garment; and does she not? Metaphors are her stuff. Examine Language. What, if you except some few primitive elements (of natural sound), what is it all but metaphors recognised as such, or no longer recognised; still fluid and florid, or now solid-grown and colourless? If those same primitive elements are the osseous fixtures in the flesh-garment, Language—then are metaphors its muscles, and tissues, and living integuments. An unmetaphorical style you shall in vain seek for: is not your very *attention** a *stretching-to* ?"

---

* *Sartor Resartus*, ch. x. Compare Heyse, s. 97. "Die gauze Sprache ist durch und durch bildlich. Wir sprechen in lauter Bildern ohne uns dessen bewusst zu sein." He gives abundant instances, classified with German accuracy. See, too, Grimm, *Gesch. d. d. Sprache*, s. 56 ff. Pott, *Metaphern vom Leben*, &c. *Zeitschr. für Vergleich. Sprachf. Jahrg.* ii. *Heft.* 2.

Our minds are simply not adapted to deal familiarly with the abstract; we yearn for the concrete, and the successful adoption of it often constitutes the power and beauty of rhetoric and poetry. For the attributes of poetry cannot better be summed up than by saying with Milton, that it is "simple, *sensuous*, passionate." It has been said, that "good writing and brilliant discourse are perpetual allegories." The Bible more than any other book abounds in this energy of style, this matchless vivacity of description; and hence of all books it is the most fresh and living, the one which speaks most musically to the ear, most thrillingly to the heart,—the one whose rich bloom of eloquence is least dimmed by being transfused into other tongues, and the rapid wings of its words the least broken and injured by the process of many hundred years. The idioms of all language approach each other most nearly in passages of the greatest eloquence and power: here the syllogism of emotion transcends the syllogism of logic, and grammatical formulæ are fused and calcined in the flame of passion.

This concreteness of style, and liberal use of simple metaphor, is nowhere so beautifully conspicuous as in the teaching of our Lord, and he

doubtless adopted it for the express purpose
that—

> They might learn who bind the sheaf,
> Or crush the grape, or dig the grave,
> And those wild eyes that watch the wave
> In roarings round the coral reef.

"Consider the *lilies how they grow; they toil
not, they spin not; and yet I say unto you that
Solomon in all his glory was not arrayed like
one of these. If, then, God so clothe the grass,
which to-day is in the field, and to-morrow is
cast into the oven, how much more will he clothe
you, oh ye of little faith!"

"Let us here adopt," says Dr. Campbell, "a
little of the tasteless manner of modern para-
phrasts, by the substitution of more general
terms, one of their many processes of infrigi-
dating, and let us observe the effect produced by
this change. 'Consider the flowers how they
gradually increase in their size; they do no manner
of work, and yet I declare unto you, that no king
whatever, in his most splendid habit, is dressed
up like them. If, then, God in his providence
doth so adorn the vegetable productions which
continue but a little time on the land, and are
afterwards devoted to the meanest uses, how

* Luke, xii. 27.

much more will he provide clothing for you!'
How spiritless* is the same sentiment rendered by
these small variations! The very particularising
of to-day and to-morrow is infinitely more expressive of transitoriness than any description
wherein the terms are general, that can be substituted in its room."

Philosophers, then, have been mistaken in com-
plaining of metaphors as a proof† of poverty.
Tropes, it has been said, would disappear, if we
had in every case a direct and independent expression, and metaphor is a coin struck only for
the earth. How this may be we know not;
although, if there be mysteries even for the
angels, then for them also will the gracious analogies of a sublime symbolism be no less necessary. For us at any rate, since it is impossible
to find a direct word for every phenomenon,

* Mr. Kingsley has compared the ancient ballad,
"Could harp a fish out of the water,
Or music out of the stane,
Or the milk out of a maiden's breast
That bairns had never nane,"
with the modern adaptation,
"O there was magic in his voice,
And witchcraft in his string!"
The expression of Herodotus about the Libyan wild asses, ἄφωτοι,
οὐ γὰρ δὴ πίνουσι, contrasts forcibly the two styles.—R. G.

† "Verborum translatio instituta est inopiæ causâ."—De
Orator. iii. 39.

metaphor is our only resource; the figure is necessitated by the non-existence of the proper term. Because poetry abounds in figures, it does not follow that it is "the dark murmur of a lie, instead of the clear cry of truth," but that it deals for the most part with thoughts which transcend the exigencies of ordinary expression. We must not complain of the lunar beam of genius, because it has not the brightness of the sun. Our choice lies between an enchanting and beautiful twilight, or a darkness which may be felt.

If any one wishes to compare the difference between metaphorical language and the phraseology which studiously avoids the use of metaphor, and clings as far as possible to bare fact, let him contrast the nomenclature of science with the parallel nomenclature of the people.

The terminology of science is of necessity " conventional,* precise, constant; copious in words and minute in distinctions, according to the needs of the science;" but this very necessity kills the imagination, and leaves an uninviting argot in the place of warm and glowing human speech. It is absurd to quarrel with and ridicule the language of science, since in its

* Dr. Whewell's *Philos. of the Inductive Sciences*, ii. 400. Mill's *Logic*, ii. ch. iv. p. 205.

researches an inaccurate or ill-defined name—
a name that *connotes* many other things, or in
itself involves an unproven theory—may be pro-
ductive of the most disastrous consequences.
But, at the same time, the mere nomenclature,
in becoming steady and determinate, is too often
uncouth and inharmonious,* and we see that if
the language of common life were equally invariable, and unelastic, imagination would be
cancelled, and genius crushed. Metaphor is no
longer possible in a language which has the
power of expressing everything. Such "lexical
superfetations" as "chrysanthemum leukanthe-
mum," and "platykeros," may be necessary to
science, but who would exchange them for the
popular names of " Reine Marguerite," and
" Stagbeetle" (*cerf volant*)? And is there not
something almost repulsive in such a term as

* Take, for instance, the botanical description of the *Hymeno-
phyllum Wilsoni;* "fronds rigid, pinnate, pinnæ recurved subuni-
lateral, pinnatifid ; the segments linear undivided, or bifid spinu-
lososerrate."—*Philosophy of Ind. Sci.* i. 165. This is the perfection of scientific terminology, but how would it answer the
purposes of common life ? And how would poetry be possible with
such clumsy terms as these ? At the same time, in *Science*, dry
precision of nomenclature is better than poetical terms like the
mediæval "flowers of sulphur." *Fancy* would only mislead in
terminology which requires accuracy ; e. g. δἴρους, the Greek name
for *jerboa* might easily have led to mistakes.

"Myosotis scorpioeides" (scorpion-shaped mouse's ear!) when compared with the sweet vulgar names "Forget-me-not," "Yeux de la Sainte Vierge," and "Plus je vous vois, plus je vous aime?" The language of science is only picturesque, when, as in the case of astronomy, it borrows from shepherd philosophers such names as the "chariot," "the serpent," "the bear," and "the milky way."

Language, then, is a plummet* which can never fathom the abysses of existence; and yet by its means we can learn more of the world of spirit than the senses can ever tell us about the visible and the material. When we speak of any sensible object, we only adopt a convenient name for a certain synthesis of properties, and we do not thereby advance a single step towards the knowledge of the thing in its abstract essence. The very existence of substance as an absolute entity, an *ens per se existens*, the postulated residuum after the abstraction of all† separate qualities which are cognisable by the senses, is entirely denied by idealists, who would reduce all outward things to a mere relation, or a modification of the sentient subject. Nature itself is with them nothing more than "an

---

* Sir Thos. Browne, *Christian Morals*, ii.
† Berkeley, *Principles of Hum. Knowledge*, xxxv.

apocalypse of the mind." We speak of "gold,"
and we mean thereby an object of which
perhaps our first and main conceptions are that
it is heavy, yellow, and valuable as a medium
of exchange; yet the property which we call
"heavy" is one which we can easily conceive
capable of modification; the property of yellow-
ness ceases when light no longer falls upon
the metal; and the property of value is one
purely conventional and continually varying.
What, then, have we left except a philosophical
figment—a something with the properties of
nothing? We cannot assert the existence of
any substance corresponding to the name "gold"
apart from these and other properties, which, as
we have seen, are mere relations. What, then,
do we really learn from language even about the
external world, the world of phenomena and of
fact? When, on the other hand, we speak of
"imagination," we name one of the noblest
faculties of the intellect, from the analogy
afforded by the property of the glassy wave,
which "refreshes and reflects" the flowers upon
its banks; yet who shall say that our metaphor
("imagination") gives us a less clear* and

* "It is remarked by a great metaphysician, that abstract ideas
are, in one point of view, the highest and most philosophical of all

definable conception than is conveyed by our general term (" gold ")?

Nothing can be known of itself, but sensible things can only be named from the manner in which they affect the senses, and things invisible can only be pictured forth analogically, from the manner in which they affect the soul. And God has given us an intellect capable of observing the analogies of which the world is full, and not only of observing them, but of applying to them with perfect comprehension the words by which we describe our physical sensations. In the wise and noble language of the son * of Sirach : " ALL THINGS ARE DOUBLE ONE AGAINST ANOTHER, AND HE HATH MADE NOTHING IMPERFECT." There is a close, though mysterious, analogy between physical and intellectual phenomena. The continual metaphors by which we compare our thoughts and emotions to the changes of the

our ideas, while in another they are the shallowest and most meagre. They have the advantage of clearness and definiteness ; they enable us to conceive and, as it were, to span the infinity of things ; they arrange, as it might be in the divisions of a glass, the many-coloured world of phenomena. And yet they are 'mere' abstractions, removed from sense, removed from experience, and detached from the mind in which they arose. Their perfection consists, as their very name implies, in their idealism ; that is, in their negative nature."—Jowett on Romans, &c., ii. 88.

* Ecclus. xlii. 23.

outer world — sadness to a cloudy sky, calm
to the silvery rays of the moonlight, anger to
waves agitated by the wind—are not, as Schel-
ling observed, a mere play of the imagination,
but are an expression in two different languages
of the same thought of the Creator, and the one
serves to interpret the other. " Nature is visible
spirit, spirit invisible nature." It could have
been no result of accident, no working of blind
chance, that made the mind of man a mirror of
the things whereby he is surrounded, and that
created the world of matter under the guidance
of laws which are an exact analogon of the laws
of mind. Thus the Universe itself, with all that
it contains, is a mighty emblem, and man is the
analogist who, by the Word that lighteth him, is
enabled to decipher it.

> Two worlds are ours : 'tis only sin
> Forbids us to descry
> The mystic heaven and earth within
> Plain as the sea and sky.

The stars and the mountains, the oceans and
winds, may exist for nobler and sublimer purposes than " to furnish man with the dictionary
and grammar of his municipal speech," but for *us*
at least it should be our first and chief cause of
thankfulness to God when we commemorate the

glories of the world in which he has placed us,
that it is by the reflection of those glories that
we grow conscious of ourselves, exactly as it is
by the reverberation of a luminous ray that
we become aware of the presence of holy
Light.

But, in those primeval ages which saw the
birth of language, the instinctive perception of
this harmony, and the application of the perceived analogy to the purposes of language, was
far more quick and vivid than it can be now,
when our minds are obscured by discussion,
dried up by logic, and too often choked by the
unnecessary gold of a vocabulary inexhaustible
and ready made. "As we go back in history,"
says Mr. Emerson, "language becomes more
picturesque, until its infancy, when it is all
poetry; or all spiritual facts are represented by
natural symbols." To the primal man his words
were like the fragments of coloured glass in the
kaleidoscope, readily admitting of a thousand
new uses, "changing their place and their effect
with every emotion which agitated his language,
and lending themselves with a lustre ever-new
to all the new combinations of his thought."

The dawn of language took place in the bright
nfancy, in the joyous boyhood of the world; the

glory-clouds still lingered among the valleys, upon the hills, and those splendors of creative power which had smitten asunder the mists that swathed the primeval chaos had not yet ceased to quiver in the fresh and radiant air. Everything was new; the soil was clad in the vernal luxuriance of green and untrodden herbage, and a blissful innocence gave to the new child of Heaven a life of "happy yesterdays and confident to-morrows." He looked at all things with the large open eyes of childish wonderment, and the * simplest facts of the eternal Order were to him miraculous events. To him "the warmth, the west wind, the ornaments of springtide returned unforeseen, and the sunrise, was but a long phenomenon which might in the morning fail the longings of night. If an arch of resplendent colours unfolded itself from heaven to earth, and there broke into a shower of brilliant atoms, sowing the soil with a dust of precious stones, it announced a message and a promise of God. If the moon disappeared in an eclipse, it was devoured by a black dragon; the thunder was the wrath of the Almighty, and the manna was his bread. The adolescent race had all the delicacy of tact, and all the freshness of sentiment, which

* Nodier, p. 59 sqq.

in youthful souls identifies itself with the poetry
of things.   In fact, life was itself a poesy full of
mystery and full of grace."

And this delicacy of tact, this youthfulness of
sensation, this ever-fresh capacity for that wonder
which is the parent of all knowledge and all
thought, was allied most closely to religion and to
poetic insight.   " They seem to me," says Plato,[*]
" to frame a right genealogy, who make Iris the
daughter of Thaumas."

> Upon the breast of new-created earth
> Man walked ; and when and wheresoe'er he moved,
> Alone or mated,—solitude was not.
> He heard, borne on the wind, the articulate voice
> Of God, and Angels to his sight appeared
> Crowning the glorious hills of Paradise ;
> Or through the groves gliding like morning mists
> Enkindled by the sun.   He sate and talked
> With winged messengers who daily brought
> To his small island in the ethereal deep
> Tidings of joy and love.   From those pure heights
> (Whether of actual vision, *sensible*
> *To thought and feeling, or that in this sort*
> *Have condescendingly been shadowed forth*

---

[*] Ἔοικεν ὁ τὴν Ἴριν Θαύμαντος ἔκγονον φήσας οὐ κακῶς γενεα-
λογεῖν.—Plato, *Theæt.* p. 155.
> " La maraviglia
> Dell ignoranza e la figlia
> E del sapere
> La madre."

Communications spiritually maintained,
And intuitions moral and divine)
Fell human kind—to banishment condemned
That flowing years repealed not.

For what is religion but reverence, and love, and worship ?   And what is poetry but the delicate perception of new truths, and new relations—the eloquent * soliloquy of wonder and of thought? "In wonder † all philosophy began ; in wonder it ends ; and admiration fills up the interspace. But the first wonder is the offspring of ignorance ; the last is the parent of adoration.   The first is the birth-throe of our knowledge ; the last is its euthanasy and apotheosis."

To the early language nothing was common or unclean, as to the youthful nations nothing was vulgar.   With them it was no degradation for a king to labour in his vineyard and tend his flocks, or for a princess to join her maidens in washing the palace-clothes.   Homer describes the cooking of a dish or the cleansing of a chamber with the same minute circumstantiality, with the same lively yet dignified delight, with the same sense that everything human has its own divine side, as he describes the falling of a hero, or the

* Mr. Mill was the first to point out the soliloquizing character of poetry.—*Essays and Dissertations.*
† Coleridge, *Aids to Reflection.*

armour of a god.   And the feeling which inspired
him with this catholicity of admiration for every
human action was a right and noble one; it was
the same feeling which actuated the Christian
poet in the quaint lines—

> A servant in this cause
>   Makes service half divine ;
> Who sweeps a room as for thy laws
>   Makes that, and the action, fine.

It is only in the fastidious conventionality of later
ages that a false shame quenches enthusiasm, and
"the quotidian ague of frigid impertinences"
infects the healthy veins of our mental constitution.   Then it is that reverence perishes, and
simple acts must be veiled in metaphysical eu-
phuisms, and simple thoughts overlaid with
galimatias, with tortured acceptations, with uncouth archaisms.   'It* must always be the same.
After the beautiful period of Spanish literature
come Gongora and his *cultorists;* after Tasso
and Ariosto, the Chevalier Marin and his pale
cortége of mannered *seicentisti,* armed with points
and conceits ; after Shakspeare, *euphuism;* after
the admirable French of the sixteenth century,
after the language of Rabelais, of Des Periers,
of Marot, of Henri Estienne, of Amyot, of

* Nodier.

Montaigne, comes "préciosité,"* so vain, so
affected, so puerile, so pretentious, so unreal,
so false.'

Thus the language of nations is the type of
their moral as well as of their intellectual character. As long as men are noble and simple,
their language will be rich in power and truth;
when they fall into corruption and sensuality,
their words will degenerate into the dingy and
miserable counters, which have no intrinsic value,
and only serve as a worthless and conventional
medium of exchange. In the pedantry of Statius,
in the puerility of Martial, in the conceits of
Seneca, in the poets who could go into emulous
raptures on the beauty of a lap-dog, and the
apotheosis of a eunuch's hair, we read the hand-
writing of an empire's condemnation. Even a
past † literature is full of power to save a people
from utter degeneracy. It is the true poet after
all who, more than the financier, more than the
merchant, more than the statesman, more than

* See *Précieuse and Précieuses* par Ch. L. Livet. 12°, 1860.
Masson's *Introduction to French Literature*, ch. iv.

† "And the regeneration of a people is always accompanied by
a rekindled interest in its early literature." We can hardly over-
rate the effect produced by the publication of Bishop Percy's
Reliques, and much may be hoped from the reproduction of the
old romancers, &c., in Spanish, of late years.

the soldier, saves his countrymen from ruin,
elevates their conduct by purifying their thoughts,
keeps their feet upon the mountain, and turns
their eyes towards the sun.

> We must be free or die, who speak the tongue
> That Shakspeare spoke, the faith and morals hold
> That Milton held !

CHAPTER VII.

WORDS NOTHING IN THEMSELVES.

"Credibilius est, quia præsens est eis, quantum id capere possunt, LUMEN RATIONIS ÆTERNÆ, ubi hæc immutabilia vera conspiciunt."—S. AUGUSTIN, *Ret.* i. 4.

"IT may lead us a little," says Locke, "towards the original of all our notions and knowledge, if we remark how great a dependence our words have on common sensible ideas; and how those which are made use of to stand for actions and notions quite removed from sense, have their rise from thence, and from obvious sensible ideas are transferred to more abstruse significations, and made to stand for ideas that come not under the cognizance of our senses."

So far we may seem to have been adducing a crowd of illustrations in support of this statement: for we have traced the germinal development of language from the seed and root of onomatopœia to the various ramifications of metaphor, and have seen convincing reason to

* *Essay on Human Understanding,* III. i. 5.

infer the primary origin of all words from sensible ideas.

Are we then obliged to give in our adherence to the sensational philosophy, and to believe that " Nature, even in the naming of things, unawares suggested to men the originals and principles of all their knowledge ? " Are we forced to accept the dogma that " there is nothing in the intellect, which has not previously existed in the sense ? "

Such are the questions which must now be considered, because these are the conclusions usually drawn from the premisses, which have been hitherto receiving our support. The discussion of them cannot be considered a digression, because it will lead us at least to recognise the existence of problems which are of the profoundest importance, the examination of which must always bear reference to the facts of language, and especially to its origin and history. The space devoted by Locke to the development of his views on the use and abuse of words is a sufficient proof that we are not wilfully turning aside from the direct discussion of the subject before us. Indeed, it is the assertion of one of Locke's acutest* and most admiring disciples, that the

---

* Horne Tooke, Part I. ch. ii.

whole of the Essay on the Human Understanding is "little more than a philosophical account of the first sort of abbreviations in language."

Before we reject the conclusion which may seem to have been involved in the facts which we have endeavoured to establish, it may be well to mark the full consequences which the sensationalists were gradually led to adopt. Locke, in defining the source of our ideas, had distinctly acknowledged an *internal sense,* which he calls reflection, as being necessary to complement the work of sensation; in the very passage which we quoted at the commencement of this chapter, he goes on to say that we have " no ideas at all, but what originally came *either* from sensible objects without, *or what we feel within ourselves from the inward workings of our own spirits of which we are conscious to ourselves within.*" Similarly, Bishop Berkeley, in his Theory of Vision, very clearly lays down "that there are properly no ideas or passive objects in the mind but what are derived from sense, *but there are, besides these, her own acts and operations ;*—such are notions."

But of that element of our thoughts which he called reflexion, Locke, although he barely asserted its existence, made so little use that it hardly counteracted the general tendency of his philosophy. "When* a term so wide and vague, or so complex and multifarious, so thin and shadowy, or so ponderous and unmanageable, as this 'reflexion' is introduced side by side with the clear, bodily, definite realities of the senses (sensation), it can hardly hold its place securely as a philosophical term." Accordingly we are not surprised to find that Locke was claimed as the founder† of a sensationalist school, whose ultimate conclusions his calm and pious mind would have indignantly repudiated.

But it was in France that the Essay on Human Understanding was received with the most enthusiastic applause; and when the metaphysics of Locke had once "crossed the channel on the light and brilliant wings of Voltaire's imagination," sensationalism reigned for a long period without a rival near the throne. Etienne de Condillac was the philosopher who was mainly instrumental in introducing to his countrymen the speculations of the great English thinker; and it is an interesting fact that in Condillac's first work, "L'Essai sur l'Origine des Connais-

---

* Dr. Whewell, *Hist. of New Phil. in Eng.* p. 72.

† We consider this on the whole a less objectionable term than "sensualist" or "sensuist;" the latter word is uncouth, and the former, from the things which it connotes, is hardly fair.

sances Humaines," 1746), he had not yet thought of "simplifying" Locke's system, by discarding reflexion as an element of knowledge. But eight years after, in his "Traité des Sensations," he states, in the broadest possible manner, that the senses are the source not only of our knowledge, but even (monstrous as it may appear) of our *intellectual faculties* themselves! And as he makes the faculty of speech the principle of superiority of men over animals, he is involved in the vicious* circle of considering language to be, at the same time and in the same sense, a cause and an effect of thought. This system found its most wonderful illustration in the too-famous description of the statue-man; a being, who, so far from being capable of acquiring memory, and judgment and thought, would even be incapable of *anything*, except mere organic impressions,† because it could have had no will whereby to contrast its personality with the action of external causes.

So far is it from being true, that there is nothing in the intellect which has not previously

---

* See V. Cousin, *Cours d'Histoire de la Phil. Morale.*

† οὔτε τῆς ψυχῆς ἴδιον τὸ αἰσθάνεσθαι οὔτε τοῦ σώματος.—Arist. *de Somno*, i. 5. "Sensation is not an affection of mind alone, nor of matter alone, but of an animated organism, i.e. of mind and matter united."—Mansell's *Metaphysics*, p. 92.

been in the sense, that even our conception of
matter* itself is derived from a superior source,
and would without the intellect be one at which
we could not arrive.   The senses themselves can
tell us nothing except in so far as they are " the
scribes† of the soul."

It might have been thought that sensationalism
itself could go no farther than Condillac, but it
found exponents still more audacious in Helvetius
and St. Lambert.   According to the former, man
is merely an animal superior to other animals
because of the greater perfection of the organs
with which he has been endowed; according to
the latter, man, when born, is only an organised
sensible mass; and the first objects which strike
our senses give us our first ideas, until thus,
gradually, Nature has created the soul within us.
We are hardly surprised after this to find that
Helvetius considers love to be only the feeling of

* "Il n'y a rien dans l'intelligence qui ait passé par les sens;
rien, pas même l'idée des sens!"—Charma, *Essai sur le Langage*,
p. 34.   This is far truer than the assertion of D'Alembert, that
" the object of Metaphysics is to examine the origin of ideas, and
to prove that they all come from our sensations."—*Elém. de
Philos.* p. 143.

† Ἡ μνήμη ταῖς αἰσθήσεσι συμπίπτουσα εἰς ταὐτόν. . .φαίνονταί
οι σχεδὸν οἶον γράφειν ἡμῶν ἐν ταῖς ψυχαῖς τότε λόγους.—Plat.
ʾΑιlebus, p. 192.

a need, courage to be the fear of death (!), and
" Do what is useful" to be the moral rule; and
that St. Lambert avows openly, that pleasure and
pain are the masters of man, so that the object of
life will be to seek the one, and avoid the other.

Are we obliged by our theory respecting the
origin of language to accept any of these conclusions?   Must we say, with Condillac, that
"science is only a well-constructed language?"
or with M. Destutt de Tracy, that "thought* is
sensation?" or (to go back to the cradle of these
materialist imaginings), must we believe, with the
old sophist, that "man† is the measure of all
things?" that there is no eternal right or truth?
that justice and turpitude are the result not of
divine instinct, but of association, habit, custom,
convention?   Must all morality be founded, with
Occam,‡ on the result of an arbitrary decree? and
must we believe, with Horne Tooke, that truth is
simply and purely relative, since its derivation is
supposed to imply that it is merely what one
" troweth?"

* Penser c'est sentir.

† πάντων μέτρον ἄνθρωπος.—Protagoras.

‡ We allude to his monstrous hyperbole "that it would be our
duty to hate God if bidden to do so by Him," which is merely
equivalent to the sycophant's excuse, πᾶν τὸ πραχθὲν ὑπὸ τοῦ
κρατοῦντος δίκαιον.

To establish such conclusions was the direct object of Horne Tooke in his "Diversions of Purley," * and it is astonishing that he should have met with such complete success. A certain Dutchman † had preceded him in the same line of argument; abusing the fact that the terms of theology, morals, and metaphysics, are originally derived from material images, he turned theology and the Christian faith into ridicule in a little Dutch dictionary, in which he gave to words, not such definitions as usage demands, but such as seemed to carry a malignant inference drawn from the original meaning; and since he had shown marks of impiety elsewhere, they say that he was punished for it in the Raspel-Huyss.

Far different was the acceptance given to the "Diversions of Purley," which to this day is praised and quoted, although a recent philologist has not scrupled to affirm that Tooke's "alluring ‡ speculations will not bear the light of advancing

* On the title of Horne Tooke's treatise, "Winged Words, or Language not only the Vehicle of Thought, but the Wheels," see Coleridge, *Aids to Refl.* p. xv.

† Leibnitz, *Nouv. Ess.* The passage is quoted by Dr. Donaldson, *New Crat.* ch. iii., where the reader will find some admirable remarks on the subject of this chapter.

‡ Mr. Wedgwood's *Etym. Dict.* p. ii.

knowledge, and it *is hardly too much to say that there is not a sound etymology in the work.*" No one has done more to overthrow his baseless fabric than the late Mr. Garnett,* in an article on English Lexicography, who has shown in particular that the details of his much-vaunted analysis of the particles may be contested more often than admitted, and indeed that his theory contains very little that can be safely relied upon. Tooke seems to have been led to his system by the conjecture that "if" is equivalent to "gif," an imperative of the verb "to give;" but as the cognate forms in other languages prove that this particle has no connection whatever either with the verb "to give" or with any other verb (a fact which was proved by Dr. Jamieson in his Scottish Dictionary), "any system founded on this basis is a mere castle in the air." "According to Plutarch," says Mr. Garnett, "the Delphian EI supported the tripod of truth; we fear that Tooke's *if imperative* led him into a labyrinth of error."

Again, let us take the etymology by which Tooke endeavours to explode the common notion of truth. He assumes that the word 'truth' is merely a contraction of "troweth," and that "trow" simply denotes to *think* or *believe.*

* *Essays*, p. 18 seqq.

The inferences are as follows: "Truth* supposes mankind; for whom and *by* whom alone the word is formed, and *to* whom alone it is applicable. If no man, then no truth. There is no such thing as eternal, immutable, everlasting truth, unless mankind, *such as they are at present*, be also eternal, immutable, and everlasting. Two persons may contradict each other, and yet both speak truth, for the truth of one person may be opposite to the truth of another." Here we are removed at once from the solid basis of certainty and conviction to the shifting deserts and treacherous waves of conjecture and doubt; and the etymologist would reduce morality and religion to shadowy superstructures built upon moving and trembling sands. Even if the derivation were admissible we should reject the conclusion, but the etymology is as erroneous as the inference drawn from it is dangerous and false. Mr. Garnett, with infinitely more probability, derives truth "from the Sanskrit *dhru*, to be established — *fixum esse;* whence *dhruwa*, certain, *i.e., established;* German, *trauen*, to rely, trust; *treu*, faithful, true; Anglo-Saxon, *treow* — *treowth* (*fides*); English, *true, truth*. To these we may add Gothic, *triggons;*

* *Diversions of Purley,* Part II. ch. v.

Icelandic, *trygge ; (fidus, securus, tutus)*: all from the same root, and all conveying the same idea of stability or security. *Truth*, therefore, neither means what is *thought* nor what is *said*, but that which is *permanent, stable*, and is and ought to be *relied upon*, because, upon sufficient data, it is capable of being demonstrated or shown to exist. If we admit this explanation, Tooke's assertions . . . . *become Vox et præterea nihil.* In all inquiries after truth, the question is, not what people, who may or may not be competent to form an opinion, *think* or *believe*, but what *grounds* they have for believing it." *

The question how mind can be affected by matter has in all ages been a problem of philosophy. Descartes accounted for it by occasional causes; Leibnitz, by pre-established harmony; Malebranche, by a vision of all things in God; Kant, by the existence of innate ideas. However the question be resolved, it is closely analogous to the question, 'how can things immaterial† and unsubstantial like thought and conception be represented, and for all practical purposes adequately represented by things physical, *i.e.,* by pulsations and modifications of the ambient air?'

* *Essays,* p. 28.　　　† See Vinet, *Essais,* p. 349.

Idealism denies the existence of an external world, and obtrudes on us in its stead " a world of spectres and apparitions ; " materialism denies us the possession of any ideas but those which we have derived from sense, and thus deprives us of all belief in an eternal and pre-existing truth; between the two we lose alike "the starry heaven above, and the moral law within." But neither of these systems can derive any real support from the phenomena of language, which indeed in no way affect the considerations they involve. For if confessedly our words have nothing to tell us, and *can* tell us nothing about the world of phenomena, and yet the common sense of mankind forces us to believe in the existence of that outer world, then it can be no argument against the existence of *noumena, i.e.,* against the existence of eternal ideas and necessary truths, that the words which we apply to our conceptions of immaterial entities are borrowed from the analogy which those conceptions offer to the objects surrounding us in the world of sense. " When we impose on a phenomenon of the physical order a moral denomination, we do not thereby spiritualise matter ; and because we assign a physical denomination to a moral phenomenon, we do not materialise spirit. Let us not from these appellations, more or less inexact, draw conclusions either as to the nature of our ideas or the essence of things."

Even if it were possible that we could invent names for each separate particle of matter in the material universe, we should *know* nothing of any one particle except that it *causes* (or, perhaps, we ought to say no more than that it *is*) a modification of ourselves; and yet we believe that there is a non-ego entirely and wholly independent of the ego, though it may in no way *resemble* our notions respecting it. Why then may we not equally believe in the independent absolute existence of ideas which correspond to our terms, — truth and justice, goodness and beauty, space and time ?

A shower falls while the sun is shining, and we are conscious of a sensation which presents to us an arch shining with the divided perfection of seven-fold light to which we have given the name Rainbow. But what does the name teach us of the thing itself ? It is not even a name for the thing itself, but only for the effect it produces upon us ; indeed for us, the very existence of the object *is* its perception, "its *esse* is *percipi*." Not

* Kant, quoted by Chalybäus, *Speculative Philosophy*, Tr. Tulk. p. 31.

only is the coloured arch a phenomenon existing
merely for us and our visual sense, but the very
raindrops are only empirical phenomena, and
" their * round shape—*nay, even the space in
which they are formed,* are nothing in themselves
but a mere modification or principle of our sensuous intuition ; with all this, however, the object
itself remains to us completely unknown." We
cannot even say that our conception of the object
is in any way like the object itself : can pain, for
instance, resemble the pricking of a pin ? Such
language, as Bp. Berkeley showed long ago, is a
mere contradiction in terms ; for " an idea can
be like nothing but an idea ; a colour or figure
can be like nothing but another colour or figure.
I appeal to any one whether it be sense to
assert that a colour is like something which is
invisible ; hard or soft, like something which is
intangible."

    What, then, is the word (*e. g.* rainbow) to us ?
In itself it is worthless, a mere hieroglyphic,
which cannot even teach us one iota about the

----

    * "There still remains the question, ' Do things as they are
resemble things as they are conceived by us ?'—a question which
we cannot answer either in the affirmative or in the negative ; for
the denial, as much as the assertion, implies a *comparison* of the
two," (which is impossible, if they are absolutely unknown).
Mansell's *Metaphysics,* p. 354.

phenomenal world. We are very far from agreeing with the " divers philosophers " mentioned by Sir Hugh Evans in the Merry Wives* of Windsor, who "hold that the lips is parcel of the mind." We still believe that objects *do* exist in the external world, even although it be absurd to say that they *resemble* our "ideas" of them. Although to *us* they can only exist as "ideas," and not as objects, we do not therefore deny that they *have* a real independent existence of their own. And precisely in the same way, whatever may be the derivation of the word truth, and however much our conceptions of that word must be modified by the laws of thought, we yet believe, as firmly as we believe anything, that truth *has* an independent, eternal, immutable existence; that it is infinitely more than a mere "*flatus vocis*;" that its indestructible idea, its original, its antetype, exists in the Divine† mind, and that if man and the works of man were to sink for ever into annihilation in the flames of a fiery surge, truth and wisdom would still exist, even as they existed when God prepared the

---

* Act I. sc. iv.

† This was the ground taken both by Plato and Aristotle in refuting the Sophists. See *Theætet.* p. 176. Arist. *Eth. Nic.* v. 7. Aristoph. *Nub.* 902 (quoted by Mr. Mansell, *Metaphysics*, p. 387).

M

heavens, "from the* beginning, or ever the earth was."

There is then no reason to complain of the materialism of language, or to be afraid of the conclusions which nominalists like Horne Tooke and his Dutch predecessor would willingly draw from the origin of words. No system of materialism will account for grammar, that *form* of language which is due to the pure reason. No treatise on the history of words will be able to point to any external source as sufficient to account for the relation† of words among themselves. No language is a *mere* collection of words; and Locke in all that he has written about *words* has offered no proof that any system of *syntax* is ultimately due to sensible ideas. His followers have attempted this, but they have failed. An eminent modern scholar has observed that a " careful‡ dissection of the whole body of inflected speech will make it plain, that while words are merely outward symbols, designating certain notions of the mind, those notions do not

---

* See Proverbs, ch. viii. 22. Jewish philosophy reaches its most passionate and eloquent strains in the expansion and inculcation of this belief. Ecclus. passim.

† See Victor Cousin, *Cours de l'Hist. de Phil. Mor.* iii. p. 214 seqq.

‡ Dr. Donaldson, *ubi sup.*

stand related in all cases, just as the words or
inflections which express them, and that we
cannot by means of mere words convert into
physical truth all that is logically and meta-
physically true."

Language is not what it has been called, "la
pensée * devenue matière." The very expression
involves a contradiction. Words *can* be nothing
but symbols, and, at the best, very imperfect
ones. To make the symbol in any way a mea-
sure·of the thought, is to bring down the infinite
to the measure of the finite. Our words mean
far more than they express, they shadow forth
far more than it is in their power to define.
When two men converse their words are but an
instrument; the speaker is descending from†
thoughts to words, the listener rising from words
to thoughts. Onomatopœia and ·metaphor are
sufficient to provide us with the material part of
language, the articulate *sounds;* but to translate
those sounds into signs or words is the effort of
a faculty which transcends the sense. On the
one hand we have a spiritual perception,‡ the
thought; on the other hand a material accident,
the combination of articulate utterances;—but

* Vinet, p. 349.
† See Harris, *Hermes,* iii. 4.   ‡ Charma, p. 64.

x 2

what power can bridge the abysm between the
two? The reason, and the reason only. Without reason, the use of metaphor would be
impossible, and the result of imitation would
be a collection of sounds as meaningless as
the screams of a parrot or the chatterings of
an ape.

Surely these considerations are sufficient to
show that there is no danger to true philosophy
in the inferences to which language leads us.
But, indeed, the whole of nominalism rests on a
vast *petitio principii*. Because our primitive
vocabulary is deduced solely from corporeal or
sensible images, it is assumed, *per saltum*, that
our intellect only admits of conceptions directly
derived from the agency of the senses, and that
therefore thought is nothing but sensation. But
the *consciousness* of the metaphor has vanished
for ages from language, and when we use such a
word as "spirit," we do not even remember that
our word means in itself no more than "a whisper
of the wind." Our primitive conceptions admitted only of *expression* by means of a material
analogy:—this is the sole ground of nominalism,
and it will not bear the enormous structure of
inferences built upon it; 1st, that our conceptions
were themselves originally material; and, 2ndly,

that they are and must be so still, because we are incapable of any others.

Finally, there are in every language " a vast number of words which may be explained by the idea, although the idea cannot be discovered by the word, as is the case with whatever belongs to the mystery of the mind." Such words are sacrifice, sacrament, mystery, eternity. The conclusion to which they lead us is a plain one, and it is one which will render us fearless of the arguments which the sensational philosophy has so long paraded with triumph as the main support of its unbeliefs. It is that " Words are at most intellectual symbols, and symbols are, at the best, words. Neither the words of language, nor the symbols of religion, are the basis and reality of thought or of worship; *they have no reality but in reason and conscience,* and are of no use but in so far as they express this reality, and are so* understood and applied."

* Bunsen's *Outlines,* ii. 146. The whole chapter is well worthy of attentive study, for the profound and noble thoughts which it contains.

CHAPTER VIII.

THE LAWS OF PROGRESS IN LANGUAGE.

THE history of almost every language points to the action of certain general laws of progress, which laws are psychological as well as linguistic, *i.e.* they correspond and are parallel to the growth and progress of the human mind. They may be briefly summed up by saying that languages advance from exuberance to moderation, from complexity and confusion to grammatical regularity, and from synthesis to analysis. The explanation and illustration of these laws will occupy the present chapter.

1st. *Languages advance from exuberance to moderation, by eliminating superfluities.*

The earliest languages are marked by exuberance,* indetermination, extreme variety, uncontrolled liberty. They are melodious, but prolix and measureless. Words were invented independently, spontaneously, as they were required by the tribe or the individual, with little or no

---

* Renan, p. 108.   Grimm, 37.

reference to already existing forms. The absence
of literature, the want of political unity, the
habits of a nomadic life, tended to create an
immense multitude of terms and idioms. Among
semi-barbarous and wandering communities the
peculiarities which we call dialects existed simultaneously and side by side.

The Caucasus and Abyssinia present us a
number of distinct languages in a narrow district·
The number and variety of the American dialects
is almost as great as that of the several tribes;
and in Oceania it has been asserted that nearly
every island or group of islands possesses a
speech which barely offers any affinity with that
of the neighbouring groups.

Unity of speech is the result of civilisation,
and it is preceded by a diversity of forms which
subsequently become the characteristics of particular localities. The steps towards unity are
three; first, we have the confused, simultaneous
existence of dialectic varieties; then the isolated
and independent existence of dialects; and,
finally, the fusion of these varieties in a more *
extended unity. Thus the earliest Hebrew
records contain traces of idioms which were subsequently the peculiar property of Aramaic, and

* Renan, p. 185.

we find in the Homeric poems a thousand
variations of form and structure which were
afterwards exclusively Æolic, or Attic, or Doric.
The explanation of this fact is to be found in the
consideration that these forms were in Homer's
time the common property of the old Ionic
tongue, and it was not till after ages that they
became appropriated and localised. The supposition that the rhapsodists employed a judicious
selection of idioms, and made a mosaic out of
distinct dialects, has long ago been abandoned
as impossible and absurd.

The process of eliminating superfluities is
found in every language. Redundancy seems to
have been necessary to an early stage of thought,
for we find it not only in words but in expressions. The whole of Hebrew poetry depends
on a repetition and enforcement of the same
fundamental thought, so as to gain emphasis and
variety. In children we find a tendency to repeat
the same thing twice, once affirmatively and once
negatively, as though the double assertion gave
them an additional security. "It is not you,
but I;" "This letter is not A, but B;" are turns
of expression well known to those who have
observed the language of the nursery. It is
surprising to find the same unnecessary tautology

existing very widely in the most advanced literatures. "We have seen with our eyes and heard
with our ears," is a superfluity which has many
types in the sacred writers; "They were in great
numbers, not in small," is the translation of a
line in the Œdipus Tyrannus, and we find even
a poet of our own times writing—

> There saw he where some careless hand
> O'er a DEAD[*] *corpse* had heaped the sand.

There is no doubt that such tautologies are often
so far from being barren, that they give force
and precision to the conception which they
convey; but the mischief of them is that they
give rise to a thousand errors of reasoning, and
to many minds have the effect of an argument.

> The Spanish fleet you cannot see, because
> It is not yet in sight,

or,

> Et respondeo
> Quia sit in eo
> Vis quæ faciat homines dormire.

might be used as the satirical motto of many a
treatise both in science and metaphysics.[†]

---

[*] Cf. 2 Kings, xix. 35. Such expressions as "a bullock that
hath horns and hoofs" belong not so much to this tendency to
avoid all possibility of mistake, as to the desire for something
graphic—the πρὸ ὀμμάτων ποιεῖν.

[†] "L'opium endormit parce qu'il a une vertu soporifique."

There are two processes by which nations get
rid of words which are mere synonyms of other
words, and are therefore burdensome. The one
is to drop altogether the superfluous word, or
only retain some one form or application of it;
the other is to desynonymise words by using
them each with one special shade of signification.
Thus, when the Greek language obtained the
word χρύσος to mean " gold," it dropped altogether the word αὖρον, which at one time it must
have possessed, as is clear from a comparison of
the word θήσαυρος with the Latin *aurum*. What
are called anomalous declensions and conjugations
are explicable in the same manner, since ancient
idioms are always richer than those which have
undergone the revision of grammarians. It is,
in fact, one of the duties of grammarians to make
a choice among the riches of popular language,
and to eliminate all words that are unnecessary.
Thus a boy would be naturally puzzled by being
told that φέρω, οἴσω, ἤνεγκα are parts of the same
verb, but it will be easy for him to understand
and remember that these words are, in fact, the

e. g. When the essence of gold and its substantial form was said to
consist in its *aureity*, the attempt at philosophic explanation was
no whit superior to those quoted in the text. The word "aureity"
was merely an effort of abstraction, but it was supposed to answer
all questions and solve all doubts.

débris of three entirely separate conjugations, parts of which only have been retained, while the remaining forms have been dropped because they were in no way needed. Merely capricious varieties have all been solved into a single verb.

2ndly. *Languages advance from confusion to regularity, from indetermination to grammar.*

What is true of the vocabulary of a language is no less true of its grammar. Here also simplicity is due to reflection, and is posterior to the rich complexity of a faculty spontaneously exercised. Scientific grammar is a subsequent invention; at their birth languages are lawless and irregular. The reason why the oldest and least grammatical languages appear to have the longest grammars, is because the anomalies are all catalogued as though they were so many rules, and what was once permissible because it then violated no law of language is ranked as the recognised exception to a definite order. An Isaiah would have been amazed at reading the innumerable rules of language by which modern grammarians suppose him to have been governed; and a Thucydides would have been hardly less astonished to see his "syllogism of passion" rigidly reduced to a syllogism of grammar.

At first, until usage had arisen, every body seems to have been at liberty to invent or adopt conjugations and declensions almost at his own caprice. "The more barbarous a language," says Herder, "the greater is the number of its conjugations." It has been a fatal mistake of philology to suppose that simplicity is anterior to complexity: simplicity is the triumph of science, not the spontaneous result of intelligence. The Basque language, which has retained much of the primitive spirit, has eleven moods; the Caffir language has upwards of twenty. Agglutination or Polysynthetism[*] is the name which has been invented for the complex condition of early language, when words follow each other in a sort of idyllic and laissez-aller carelessness, and the whole sentence, or even the whole discourse, is conjugated or declined as though it were a single word, every subordinate clause being inserted in the main one by a species of *incapsulation.* This is the case with the Aztec, the languages of the Pacific, and many other languages. The Mongol declines an entire firman, and even in Sanskrit, flexions so far supersede syntax that the whole

---

[*] First used by M. Duponceau in his English translation of the German Grammar of Zeisberger. Charma, p. 266. Schleicher called these languages "Holophrastic."

THE ORIGIN OF LANGUAGE.

thought is in some sort declined. In Mexican, the word *Notlazomahiuzteopixcatatzin*, with which they salute the priests, is easily decomposed into " Venerable priest, whom I honour as my father ;" and in Turkish,† the single word *Sev-ish-dir-il-me-mek* means "not to be brought to love one another." Yet even these are entirely surpassed by some of the dialects of North America. In the ‡ Iroquois, for instance, one word of twenty-one letters expresses this sentence of eighteen words : " I give some money to those who have arrived, in order to buy them more clothes with it." This one word is an agglomeration of simple words and roots in a violent state of fusion and apocope.

3rdly. Analogous in great measure to the law which we have been mentioning (or perhaps we may say a further development of the same law), is the progress of language *from Synthesis to Analysis.*

We have seen that many ancient languages are

* Humboldt, quoted by Charma, p. 222.
† Max Müller, p. 113. Compare Molière, *Le Bourgeois Gentil-homme*, iv. 4. "Mons. Jourdain : *Tant de choses en deux mots !—*. Cov.: Oui, la langue turque est comme cela, elle dit beaucoup en peu de paroles."
‡ Ampère, *Rev. des Deux Mondes*. Fevrier, 1853, p. 572.

polysynthetic or * holophrastic, *i.e.*, that they produce the entire thought or sentence under the
form of one complex and rich unity, and subordinate every word and phrase to the domination of
the entire clause. Even in early Greek and
Latin we may find traces of this "*holophrasis*"
in the separation of two parts of the same word
which was permissible by what is called *tmesis*,
as for instance in such expressions as κατὰ δάκρυ
χέουσα, and even κατὰ πίονα μῆρι' ἔκηα. In Latin the
same licence is far more rare, although we find
it in the lines, "*Inque cruentatus*," &c., and it '
was retained in one or two compounds, as "*Quo te
cumque* ferent*.*" In both languages these extreme
cases early disappeared, and the startling audacity
of Ennius in the famous

Cere comminuit *brum,*

for "comminuit cerebrum," would probably have
made Virgil stare and gasp, as much as† the
modern

O *Jo* qui terras de cœlo despicis *hannes.*

But although nothing is left in the Indo-
European languages but the faint *traces* of that
sylleptical tendency which seems to have marked

---

* Also called "*incorporant.*"   † Charma, p. 223.

the earliest stage of language, they offer the most
splendid examples of a perfect synthesis.   By a
facile power of composition, and by attaching to
the verb and noun a variety of terminations
capable of distinguishing the nicest modifications
of meaning, they have produced an instrument of
thought almost unrivalled in accuracy and beauty.

In Greek and Latin one word was enough
to express alike the subject, copula, and predi-
cate ; in English, two are always requisite, and
generally three.   The single word τύπτω requires
the three words—" I am striking "—to render it;
to translate *amabor* in English or in German we
require four words, "I shall be loved—*Ich werde
geliebt werden* ;" and the same is true of many
other parts of the verb ; as ἐτετιμήμεθα, *periisses*,
" we had been honoured," " you would have
perished."

At first sight this analysis may seem to be a
defect, but, in point of fact, it is a development.
It is a bad thing for the human mind to be
subjected to the despotism of a rigid grammar,
the tyranny of too perfect a form.   As it is the
danger of advancing civilisation and of too
refined a society to reduce men to the deal level
of uniformity, and subject every caprice of the
individual to the domination of an unwritten

code, called the "laws of society," so a language which crystallises every relation in a definite form tends to cramp and restrain the genius of those who use it. In the tragedies of Æschylus and the odes of Pindar, marvellous as is the power which crams every rigid phrase with the fire of a hidden meaning, we yet feel that the form is cracking under the spirit, or at least there is a tension injurious to the general effect. A language which gets rid of its earlier inflections—English, for instance, as compared with Anglo-Saxon—loses far less than might have been supposed.

The progress of language from synthesis to analysis is that of the human intelligence. Later generations find the language of their ancestors too learned for their own use. For the unity, spontaneous but often obscure, of the primitive tongues, they substitute an idiom clearer and more explicit by giving a separate existence to every subject in the sentence. They break up the conglomerated jewels of old speech to reset them in an order less dazzling but more distinct. They sacrifice the magnificence of mystery to the light of distinct comprehension. Instead of one sentence, out of whose tangled intricacies flashed, all the more brightly from contrast, the rays of enthusiasm and genius, they attain to a logical accuracy which gives to each idea and each relation its isolated expression. What they lose in euphony, force, and poetic concision, they gain in the power of marking the nicest shades of thought; what they lose in* elasticity they gain in strength. If synthetic and agglutinative languages are the best instruments of imagination, analysis better serves the purposes of reflection. Splendid efflorescence is followed by ripe fruit.

It is thus† that Sanskrit, with its eight cases, six moods, and numerous inflections, capable of expressing a crowd of secondary ideas, decomposes first into the Pali (?), Prâkrit, and Kawi, dialects less rich and learned, but more precise, which substitute auxiliaries and prepositions for case and tense; and even these latter, too complex for ordinary use, are gradually displaced by the more vulgar dialects of Hindostan,—the Hindoo, the Mahrattah, and the Bengali.

In the same way the Zend, Pehlvi, and Pars-i, are replaced by the modern Persian. The Zend,

---

* Grimm, ss. 37—47.

† Renan, p. 160 seqq. It is doubtful whether the Pali was anything more than an artificial language. If so, however, it is an unique phenomenon, and it must not be forgotten that a similar opinion was once entertained respecting the Sanskrit and Zend.

with its long and complicated words, its want of
prepositions, and its method of supplying the
want by means of cases, represents a language
eminently synthetic.   Modern Persian, on the
contrary, is poorer in flexions than almost any
language which exists ; it may be said, without
exaggeration, that its whole grammar might be
compressed into a few pages.   Modern Greek is
the analysis or decomposition of ancient Greek
during a long period of barbarism. The Romance
languages are Latin submitted to the same
process ; Italian, Spanish, French, and Walla-
chian, are merely Latin mutilated, deprived of its
flexions, reduced to shortened forms, and supplying by numerous monosyllables the learned
organisation of the ancient idioms.   " The fact
then that the people in Italy, in France, in Spain,
in Greece, on the banks of the Danube and of the
Ganges, have been reduced to the necessity of
treating their ancient languages in precisely the
same manner to accommodate them to their
wants ; and the fact that two languages, so dis-
tant in time and space as the Pali and the
Italian for instance, occupy positions exactly
identical in relation to their mother-tongues,
affords the best proof that there is in the progress of languages a necessary law, and that

there is an irresistible tendency which leads idioms
to despoil themselves of an apparel too learned to
clothe a form more simple, more popular, and
more convenient." *

In the Semitic languages we find the progress
towards analysis from various † causes less decided,
but no less ascertainable.   Ancient Hebrew is
remarkable for its agglutination. "Like a child,"
says Herder, " it seeks to say all at once."   It
uses one word where we require five or six.   But
as we approach the period of the captivity we find
a propensity to replace grammatical mechanisms
by periphrasis, a propensity still more marked in
modern or Rabbinical Hebrew. The later dialects
— Chaldean, Samaritan, Syriac — are longer,
clearer, more analytic. These, in their turn, are
absorbed into Arabic, which pushes still farther
the analysis of grammatical relations.   But the
delicate and varied flexions of Arabic are still too
difficult for the rude soldiers of the early Khâlifs ;
solecisms multiply, grammatical forms are abandoned, and for the Arabic of the schools we get the
vulgar Arabic, which is simpler and less elegant,
but in some respects more accurate and distinct.

---

* Precisely the same change takes place in the growth of English
from Saxon, and Danish from Icelandic.

† *Hist. des Langues Sém.* v. 1, 2, and 3.

Even the languages of central and eastern
Asia are not entirely wanting in analogous phenomena. But the facts already adduced are amply
sufficient to prove that, in the history of
languages, Synthesis is primitive, and Analysis,
far from being the natural process of the intelligence, is only the slow result of its development.
And if it be a natural development it must, on
the whole, be considered an advance.

"An instance,"* observes Grimm, "unique but
decisive, is alone sufficient to replace all the proofs
and arguments which I have accumulated in my
reasoning on this subject.   Among modern
languages there is not one which has gained more
force and solidity than the English by neglecting
or breaking the ancient rules of sound, and
suffering almost all flexions to drop. The abund-
ance of medial sounds, the pronunciation of
which may be learnt but cannot be taught, gives
to this language a power of expression, such as
perhaps no human language has ever attained.
Its highly spiritual genius and marvellously
happy development are due to the astonishing
union of the two most noble languages in modern

* *Uber den Urspr. d. Sprache*, p. 50.   Another weighty testi-
mony to the splendour of the English language may be found in
Adelung's *Mithridates*.

Europe, German and Romance. We know the part which each of these elements plays in the English language; one of them is almost entirely devoted to the representation of sensible ideas, the other to the expression of intellectual relations. Yes, the English language, which has produced and nourished with its milk the greatest of modern poets, the only one who can be compared to the classical poets of antiquity (who does not see that I am speaking of Shakspeare ?), may of good right be called an universal language, and seems destined, like the English people itself, to extend its empire farther and farther in all quarters of the globe."

To the laws which we have been considering, many philologists would be inclined to add a fourth—viz., the *progress to polysyllabism from a state originally monosyllabic.* Many arguments may undoubtedly be adduced, which give a *primâ facie* probability to this supposition.* We will proceed briefly to state them.

It is argued, firstly, that we should have expected *à priori* a predominance of monosyllabic roots, because it is unlikely that a single powerful impression would have expressed itself by more

* See Benloew, p. 15 sqq. Humboldt, *Über die Verschiedenheit des menschlichen Sprachbaues,* ad finem.

than one sound. Since one sound would have
been sufficient, we should not be inclined to look
for any superfluity. Impression would provoke
expression with the same rapidity that the flash
of lightning is kindled by the shock of two
electric clouds. It must be remembered that the
young senses of the human race were unaccustomed to compound articulations, and neither
their ears nor their tongues would have led them
to signify by two sounds or two syllables an impression essentially single.

Secondly, it is said that existing facts prove
the likelihood of this conclusion. Thus, to this
day, some nations are unable to pronounce compound consonants by one emission of the voice.
Such is the case with the Mantschou, and the
Chinese can only utter the word *Christus* by
changing it according to the custom of his language into *ki-li-su-tu-su.** The Chinese then may
be considered as a language petrified in its first
stage of flexionless and ungrammatical monosyllabism. Thus, in order to express the plural,
they are obliged to add the words, " another "
and " much," or to repeat the noun twice, expressing " us " by " me another," and trees by " tree,†

* The Chinese 'l' is pronounced like 'r.'
† Many readers may recall the story of the late Mr. Albert

tree." The prayer, " Our Father which art in heaven," assumes in Chinese * the form " Being heaven me another (=our) Father who," a style not unlike the natural language of very young children.

Thirdly, it is asserted that all existing languages are capable of being deduced from monosyllabic roots; that even the triliteral † Semitic languages afford abundant evidence of the fact that the three consonants are only the result of a growth, since one of the consonants is often weak and unnecessary, and many of the words expressing simple ‡ ideas have only one syllable.

Whatever weight may attach to these considerations, they do not appear to be convincing. The attempt of Fürst and Delitzch to get over the fact of Semitic triliteralism is not completely successful, and no evidence has ever been

---

Smith about the Bishop being described in the mixed jargon of Hong Kong as the " A-one-heaven-business-man."

* Adelung, *Mithridates*, i. p. 412. Some deny the monosyllabic character of Chinese. (Prof. Key, Art. *Language, Engl. Cycl.*)

† It should be observed that triliteralism is not *necessarily* incompatible with monosyllabism. See *Hist. des Langues Sémitiques*, p. 94, 2nde ed.

‡ As אָב father, אֵם mother, אָח brother, הַר mountain, יָד hand, יוֹם day, &c.

adduced to show the causes which could have
influenced a language to abandon an essentially
monosyllabic character, or the time when so
immense a change could have taken place.

Chinese, as we know, has been monosyllabic
from the earliest period, and continues so to
his day; and even Thibetian and Burmese,*
though they have, under the influence of other
languages, made great efforts to attain a grammar,
have yet retained the ineffaceable impress of their
original condition. We therefore reject this
fourth law, as one which, even if possible, is by
no means proven. Further discussion of it will,
indirectly, be involved in the following chapter.
At best, it can only be regarded as an artificial
hypothesis, occasionally convenient for the purposes of the grammarian, but not corresponding
to any real condition of the languages as once
spoken.

* Renan, p. 168. I must content myself here with a general
reference to M. Renan, to whose works I have been very greatly
indebted throughout the chapter, and indeed, as I have repeatedly
observed, throughout the book.

CHAPTER IX.

THE FAMILIES OF LANGUAGES.

" Facies non omnibus una,
Nec diversa tamen, quales decet esse sororum."—VIRG.

IT has been considered by many that language
has passed through four* stages. 1. A period in
which words succeed each other in the natural
order of the thought, with nothing except this
order to express their mutual relation, and with
few or no inflections, as in Chinese. 2. A period
of agglutination in which the smaller words to
express relation have assumed an inflectional
form, but without losing the trace of their originally distinct existence, as in Mongol and the
majority of existing languages. 3. A period of
amalgamation, in which the language becomes
purely inflectional, as in Latin and Greek. 4. A
period of analysis, in which inflections fall off

---

* Pott's formula for the morphological classification of languages
was that they are "isolating," "agglutinative," and "inflectional." Professor Müller and Baron Bunsen have shown that
these divisions nearly correspond with three stages of political
development—"Family," "Nomad," and "State."

and get displaced by separate words, auxiliaries, prepositions, &c., as in English.*

That languages exist in each of these conditions is undeniable, but that they represent an historical sequence is an inference which may well be disputed.   The common *à priori* notion that complexity is a proof of development is, as we have already seen, entirely erroneous ;   since the languages of American   savages   and   central Africans are surprising in their grammatical richness, and the bald monosyllabic Chinese is yet an adequate   organ for a developed civilisation. The logical order is not the same as the historical.   It is the opinion of M. Renan that each branch of languages was, from the first, pervaded by one dominant idea, which was due to the genius of the race by which it was produced, and that, from this idea, all further changes directly derive their origin.   The entire language existed implicitly in its primitive stage, just as a bud contains entire every essential part of the full-grown flower.   Languages once monosyllabic, for instance, have, he maintains, always continued so, and although some languages of the trans-Gangetic peninsula have effected a real progress in the direction of grammatical polysyllabism,

* *Encycl. Brit. Art. Language.* (Dr. Latham.)

yet an abyss still separates them from the languages which are truly grammatical, — an abyss which, he thinks, never has been and never can be bridged over.

But we shall be better able to enter on these most important considerations when we have glanced at the *certain* results respecting the classification of languages which have been at present established by modern philology.

Two families of languages, embracing a large and widely-separated number of the spoken languages of the globe, have now been distinctly recognised and clearly defined. These are the Indo-European, and the Semitic. The remaining languages, which are non-Semitic and non-Arian, have been recently included under the general name Turanian, and the high authority of Baron Bunsen and Prof. Max Müller has secured for this name a wide acceptation. We shall see hereafter that the semblance of unity in these languages, which is assumed by the adoption of this name, has been disputed by some of the ablest philologists, and at any rate the languages of the so-called Turanian family have far less real claim to the ties of mutual relationship than the members of the Semitic and Indo-European families.

I. Of these families, the noblest and most widely-spread is the Indo-European, or as it is now more generally called, the Arian family. Neither of these names is entirely* unobjectionable, though either of them is preferable to the term Indo-Germanic, which is now abandoned as wholly inaccurate.   The name Indo-European marks the geographical extent of these languages, but it is inconvenient, and not quite wide enough. The name Arian was given them because the ancestors of the people who spoke them are supposed to have called themselves "Arya," † or nobly-born.   This name is now generally adopted, and M. Pictet, one of the profoundest of modern comparative philologists, has called his most recent work, "Les Origines Indo-Européennes ou les Aryas Primitifs."   But although this term Arya is of frequent occurrence in the later Sanskrit literature, and was also familiar to the Persians, the traces of it among the other

---

* On l'a designée par les noms de famille Indo-Germanique ou Indo-Européenne, lesquels ne sont *ni logiques ni harmonieux*, car ils n'expriment qu'imparfaitement le sens qui leur est attribué, et leur longueur démesurée en rend l'emploi fort peu commode." —Pictet's *Origines Indo-Eur.* p. 28.   They have, however, the advantage of explaining themselves.

† Burnouf, *Commentaire sur le Yaçna*, p. xciii. See also Bunsen's *Outlines*, I. 281.

branches of the race are few and dubious; they
are but very "*faint** echoes," if echoes at all, "of
a name which once sounded through the valleys
of the Himâlaya." Still it is not likely that this
name will now be superseded, as Rask's term
Japhetic involves an unwarrantable assumption;
and the name Pataric (derived from Patar,
the Sanskrit "*pitar*," a father), which has
been recently suggested,† is not likely to gain
ground.

The Arian family comprises eight divisions,
the Hindu, the Persian, Greek, Latin, Lithua-
nian, Sclavonic, Teutonic, and Celtic; of these
it is uncertain whether the Celtic or the Sanskrit
represents the oldest phase, but it is known that
all of them are the daughters of a primeval form
of language which has now ceased to exist, but
which was spoken by a yet-undivided race at a
period when Sanskrit and Greek had, as yet, only

* These traces are most ably pointed out in the *Edinburgh
Review* for October, 1851, quoted in an interesting note by Prof.
Max Müller, *Survey of Languages*, p. 28, 2nd ed. See, too, Pictet,
pp. 27—34, who connects the root *ar* with the words Erin, Elam,
Ariovistus, Arminius, oriri, &c. If this be a right derivation of
Erin, the fact is important, as showing that some memory of the
old name was preserved in the extreme West as well as in the
East.

† By a writer in the *Saturday Review* for Nov. 19, 1859.

an implicit existence. " It is," says M. Renan, [*]
" the noblest conquest of comparative philology
to have enabled us to cast a bold glance over
this primitive Arian period, when the whole
germ of the world's civilisation was concentrated
in one straight ray. Just as the Romance dialects
are all derived from a language which was once
spoken by a small tribe on the banks of the
Tiber; so the Indo-European languages presup-
pose a language spoken in a very narrow district.
What motive, for instance, could have induced all
Indo-European nations to derive the name of
'father' from the root 'pa' and the suffix 'tri'
or 'tar,' if this word, in its complete shape, had
not formed part of the vocabulary of the primitive Arians? What motive, above all, could
have induced them, after their departure, to
derive the name of 'daughter' from a notion so
special as that of *milking*[†] (Sanskrit *duhitri*,
θυγάτηρ, dochter, &c.), if this word had not
deduced the reason for its form in the manners of an ancient pastoral family?" It is
from considerations such as these that we

[*] P. 49.

[†] For a graphic sketch of early Arian life as deduced from the
records of language, see Weber's *Indische Skizzen*, pp. 9, 10;
Pictet's *Origines Indo-Européennes;* Müller's *Ess. on Comp.
Mythology.*

prove the great fact of the Indo-European unity,—the New World now thrown open to modern scholarship. "That the Sanskrit, the ancient language of India, the very* existence of which was unknown to the Greeks and Romans before Alexander, and the sound of which had never reached a European ear till the close of the last century, that this language should be a scion of the same stem, whose branches overshadow the civilised world of Europe, no one would have ventured to affirm before the rise of comparative philology. It was the generally received opinion that if Greek, Latin, and German came from the east, they must be derived from the Hebrew,—an opinion for which, at the present day, not a single advocate could be found,† while formerly to disbelieve it would have been tantamount to heresy. No authority could have been strong enough to persuade the Grecian army that their gods and their hero-ancestors were the same as those of King Porus, or to convince the English soldier that the same blood was running in his veins, as in the veins of the dark Bengalese. And yet there is not an English jury now-a-days, which,

* Müller, p. 28 sqq.
† Except some popular modern divines.

after examining the hoary documents of language,
would reject the claims of a common descent
and a legitimate relationship between Hindu,
Greek, and Teuton. Many words still live in
India and in England that witnessed the first
separation of the northern and southern Arians,
and these are witnesses not to be shaken by any
cross-examination. Though the historian may
shake his head, though the physiologist may
doubt, and the poet scorn the idea, all must
yield before the facts furnished by language.
There was a time when the ancestors of the
Celts, the Germans, the Danes, the Greeks, the
Italians, the Persians, and Hindus, were living
beneath the same roof, separate from the
ancestors of the Semitic and Turanian races."

Comparative philology enables us to form a
very probable conjecture respecting the cradle of
the Arian race, and even to draw in outline a
picture of their primitive civilisation. We know
that this race was not indigenous in India. M.
Lassen has proved that it entered India from the
north as an aristocratic and conquering nation,

---

* Lassen, *Indische Alterthumskunde.* Renan, 219 seqq.
Klaproth builds an argument for the Northern origin of the
Arians on the word "birch," which bears an analogous name
"not only in the German and Slavonic tongues, but also in the

distinguished by its fair complexion from the swarthier aborigines; and a crowd of linguistic inferences converge into a proof that it sprang from the mountain-cradle of Imüus, from which neighbourhood it seems likely that the Shemites also derived their origin.

The traditions of the Arians, as well as the facts of their language, point to Bactriana, as the region in which they first appeared; central in position, temperate in climate, rich in the metals always found in mountainous countries, resembling Europe in its flora and fauna, and equally removed from tropical luxuriance and northern

Sanskrit—*b'hurjja*. . . . It seems birch was the only tree the invaders recognised, and could name, on the south side of the Himalaya; all others being new to them. The inference may be right or wrong—it is, at all events, ingenious." Garnett's *Essays,* p.33. See Klaproth, *Nouv. J. Asiat.* v. 112. Pictet, *Orig. Ind.* i. 217. The fact that the words for oyster are derived from the same root in the European languages (Gk. ὄστρεον, Ang.-Sax. *ostra,* Irish *oisridh,* Cymr. *œstren,* Russ. *üsterstl,* French *huître,* Germ. *Auster,* &c.), but *not* in the Sanskrit or Indian branch of the Arian family,—would seem to show that there was a great separation of Eastern and Western Arians before the family had reached the shores of the Caspian. A similar fact is observed in the name for flax, (Gr. λίνον, Lat. *linum,* Goth. *lein,* Ang.-Sax. *lin,* Cym. *llin,* Russ. *lenü,* &c.), and shows that the Western Arians were the first of the family to desert pastoral for agricultural pursuits. *Id.* pp. 320, 516. Few studies are more interesting than the "linguistic palæontology," which thus enables us to revive the form of an extinct language and civilisation.

poverty, no other country could be found more
perfectly suited for the peaceable development of
the noble family which was destined to mould the
character of the world.

The Arians did not appear till late in the
world's history. 'The Achæmenid empire, which
is the first great conquering Arian empire, is
contemporary with a period when the descendants of Ham had already lost all excellence, and
when China had long arrived at that degree of
administrative absorption of which the *Tcheou-li*
affords an astonishing picture, and which has so
near a resemblance to absolute decrepitude.
Brilliant civilisations, powerful kings, organised
empires, already existed in the world at a
period when our ancestors were still a race of
poor and ignorant peasants. And yet it was
these austere patriarchs who, in the midst of
their chaste and obedient families, thanks to
their pride, their cultivation of right, and their
noble self-respect, laid the foundation of the
future. Their thoughts, their terms, were destined to become the law of the moral and intellectual world. They created those eternal words,
which, with many changing shades of meaning,
were destined to become 'honour,'* 'virtue,'
'duty.'

* Renan, p. 235.

In speaking thus of the apparition of a race
or a language, we only mean the time at which
man awoke to reflection and consciousness.
The origin of language is not *necessarily* identical (considered scientifically) with the origin
of mankind. The circumstances and conditions
under which man first appeared on the face of
the world is a subject for the research of the
physiologist, rather than the philologist, and it is
more than doubtful whether the most earnest inquiries will ever be able to draw aside the thick
veil which hides the dawn of human life. In endeavouring to derive from the facts of language
some conjecture as to the nucleus around which it
grew, and the primitive condition of the races with
whose distinctive genius it is indelibly stamped,
we are not pretending to throw any light on the
original appearance of the fathers of mankind.

II. Second in importance, although earlier
in historical development, stands the great
SEMITIC family of languages. Formerly they
were called by the general name of oriental languages, and Eichhorn was, we believe, the first to
give them their present designation. The name is,
however, defective, since many people who spoke
Semitic languages (as for instance the Phœni-
cians) were descended, according to Gen. x., from

Ham, and several mentioned in that chapter as descendants of Shem (for instance, the Elamites), did *not* speak a Semitic language. But it is now generally agreed that the sense of this document is geographical, not ethnographical, and that the name of Shem is a general term to describe the central zone of the earth. Were we to name these languages, on the analogy of the word Indo-European, from their extreme terms, we must call them Syro-Arabian. Leibnitz suggested the name Arabic, but this would be to use an objectionable synecdoche, and, on the whole, the term Semitic involves no inconvenient consequences if it be considered as purely conventional.*

The Semitic languages have been destined to exercise a stupendous influence over the religious thought of mankind. Almost unconscious of science and philosophy, this theocratic race has devoted itself to the expression of religious instincts and intuitions,—in one word, to the establishment of Monotheism. The three most widely spread and enduring forms of belief originated in the bosom of this family. They were essentially the people of God, and to them belong, *par excellence*, the psalm, and the proverb, and

* *Histoire des Langues Sém.* pp. 1, 2.

the prophecy,—the words of the wise, and their
dark sayings upon the harp. Clear but narrow in
their conceptions, marked by their subjective
character, and capable of understanding unity but
not multiplicity; they lacked alike the lofty
spiritualism of India and Germany, the keen
sense of perfect beauty which was the legacy of
Greece to the new Latin nations, and the profound yet delicate sensibility which is the dominant mark of the Celtic peoples. And yet
neither India nor Greece alone could have taught
the world the great lesson which was connected
by the Semitic race with their most imperious
instincts, that there is but one God, and that
religion is something more than a relative
conception. Destitute of that restless spirit of
inquiry which has led the sister-race to explore
every nook of the universe and every secret of
the mind, the highest attainment of Semitic
research is to declare that the increase of knowledge is the increase of sorrow, and that the
praise and service of God is the sole end and aim
of life. It was a great lesson which the world
could ill have spared, and it more than atoned
for the absence of research, of imagination, of
art, of military organisation, of public spirit, of
political life : it more than atones even for an

egotistic poetry and a defective conception of morality and duty.

The Semitic languages partake of the characteristics of that race whose thoughts they embodied. They are simple and rigid, metallic rather than fluid; physical and sensuous in their character, deficient in abstraction, and almost incapable of metaphysical accuracy. The roots are triliteral in form and so few in number that their meanings are generally vague, being in fact a series of metaphorical applications of some sensible perception. They are deficient in style and in perspective; they are, as Ewald observes, lyric and poetic, rather than oratorical and epic; they are the best means of showing us the primitive tendencies of language; they may be compared to the utterances of a fair and intelligent infancy retained in a manhood which has not fulfilled the brilliant promise of its early days.

The Semitic family has three main branches —viz., the Aramaic, divided into two dialects, Syriac and Chaldee; the Hebrew, with which is connected the Carthaginian and Phœnician, and the Arabic. Besides these the Egyptian, the Babylonian, and the Assyrian and the Berber dialects are now considered to have a Semitic character, such at least is the conclusion arrived at by those whose authority is of the highest importance—viz., Champollion and Bunsen in the case of Egyptian, M.M. Lassen and Eugène Bornon, Dr. Hincks and Sir H. Rawlinson in the case of Assyrian, and Prof. F. Newman in the case of the Berber dialects.* It is admitted, however, that the people speaking these languages were the cognate rather than the agnate descendants of Shem; and it must not be overlooked, that the conclusion which would rank these languages as indubitably Semitic is rejected by philologists so celebrated as M.M. Pott, Ewald, Wenrich, and Renan.†

III. All languages which belong to neither of these two great families have been classed together under the name of the TURANIAN, NOMADIC, or ALLOPHYLIAN family,‡ which "comprises all

---

* Müller's *Survey*, p. 23 seqq.

† *Hist. des Langues Sémitiques*, pp. 70—90.

‡ The name was suggested by Baron Bunsen in 1847. *Outlines*, i. 64. He even argues for the Turanian character of the Chinese; "although it is certain that the same opposition exists between the two as there is between inorganic and organic life." General laws, operative in the formation of all languages, ought not to be taken for indications of special affinity; who would maintain the identity of quadrupeds and birds from the analogy of their respiratory and digestive systems! In the formation of languages certain first principles were necessarily observed by all, and this of course leads to some general resemblances.

languages spoken in Asia or Europe, not included under the Arian and Semitic families,
with the exception perhaps of the Chinese and
its dialects."

The chief labourers in the field of Turanian
philology were Rask, Klaproth, Schott, and
Castren; but even M. Müller, one of the
main authorities for the classification of the
various branches of language which occupy
this wide range (*e.g.*, the Tungusic, Mongolic,
Turkic, Samoiedic, and Finnic), candidly admits
that the characteristic marks of union ascertained for this immense variety of languages,
" are *as yet very vague and general*, if compared
with the definite ties of relationship which
severally unite the Semitic and the Arian." He
argues, however, that this is exactly what we
should have expected, *à priori*, in the case of
Nomadic languages spoken over an area so vast;
languages which have never been the instruments
of political organisation, which have no history in
the past and no destiny in the future, and which
never had any literature to give fixity to their
acknowledged unsettledness. Though the " Turanian " languages occupy by far the largest portion of the earth (viz., all but India, Arabia,
Asia-Minor and Europe), there is not a single

positive principle, except perhaps agglutination, which can be proved to pervade them all.[*]

It is impossible here to examine the arguments on which the unity of this family has been considered to be *approximately* established, while it is admitted that this unity does not admit of any proof so strong and decisive as in the case of the Indo-European and Semitic families. Those who ·seek the evidence will find it stated, at full length, and with great eloquence and ability, by Prof. Max Müller, in his " Survey of Languages," and also in Baron Bunsen's " Outlines." Suffice it here to say, that to many the vast group of Turtaro-Finnic languages still appear to be purely sporadic, and to have no common character except such as is involved in their being neither Arian nor Semitic, *i.e.*, in the *purely negative trait* of an absence of certain development. Under these circumstances, we think that for the present it would be far better to call these languages by the *purely negative*

---

[*] " Turanian speech is rather a *stage* than a *form* of language ; it seems to be the form into which human discourse, naturally, and, as it were, spontaneously throws itself. . . The principle of agglutination, as it is called, which is its most marked characteristic, seems almost a necessary feature of any language in a constant state of flux and change, absolutely devoid of a literature, and maintaining itself in existence by means of the scanty conversation of Nomades."—Rawlinson's *Herodotus*, i. p. 645.

name, Allophylian,*—a name which involves no
hypothesis, and which has the advantage of being
the simple assertion of a fact.

But even supposing that we unhesitatingly
admit a postulate so large as that required of us,
by the supposition that the Nomad languages
may be united into one family, which has points
of affinity with the dialects of Africa and America,
and even with Chinese, the further and more
important question still remains; Are there any
points of osculation between the languages of
these three great distinct families? Is there any
evidence in the present state of philology sufficiently strong to induce a scientific belief in the
primitive unity of human language, and therefore
of the human race? The answer to that question
must be found in the next chapter, and I need
only premise, that it is here treated as a question
of pure science, and is entirely separated from its
theological bearings. The question before us is
not "must we believe in the unity of the human
race?" but "does philology furnish any proofs
or presumptions of the unity of the human race?"

---

* It is rather strange that this name, so peculiarly appropriate,
and so much preferable to the other, has not met with wider
acceptation. It was suggested by Dr. Prichard, "the greatest of
English ethnologists."

CHAPTER X.

ARE THERE ANY PROOFS OF A SINGLE PRIMITIVE LANGUAGE?

"Innumeræ linguæ dissimillimæ inter se, ita ut nullis machinis ad communem originem retrahi possint."—F. SCHLEGEL.

BESIDES the immense number of languages now spoken over the surface of the globe, we must remember that hundreds have now died away altogether, and left no trace behind them. Even in our own times, languages are dying out; the last person who could speak Cornish died almost within this generation,* and it is probable that Manx will not long survive, although it may be violently galvanized into a semblance of vitality. Many of the sporadic dialects, spoken by the North American Indians, have disappeared with the tribes that spoke them; and Humboldt even mentions that he had seen a parrot which was the only living thing that preserved the articulation of one forgotten

* Dolly Pentreath, the last person who could speak Cornish, died in 1770.

tongue. Every extant language has grown out of the death of a preceding one.* " Like a tree, unobserved through the solitude of a thousand years, up grows the mighty stem, and the mighty branches of a magnificent speech. No man saw the seed planted; no eye noticed the. infant sprouts; no register was kept of the gradual widening of 'its girth, or of the growing circumference of its shade, till the deciduous dialects of surrounding barbarians dying out, the unexpected bole stands forth in all its magnitude, carrying aloft in its foliage, the poetry, the history, and the philosophy of an heroic people."†

Thus the Greeks and Romans‡ displaced by their dominant idioms numerous languages of Southern and Central Europe; the Arabs effaced the indigenous dialects of a large portion of Western Asia, and Northern and Eastern Africa; the Spanish and Portuguese have expelled a crowd of American languages. Again, the Visigoths and Alani lost in Spain both their name and their language; the Ostrogoths and Heruli suffered the same fate in Italy; and in

* Bunsen, *Outlines*, ii. 92.
† Ferrier's *Institutes of Metaphysics*, p. 13.
‡ Adr. Balbi, *Atlas ethnographique. Disc. prélim.* lxxv—lxxix.

short, we may fairly suppose that the dead languages of the world are nearly as numerous as those that are still living.

Passing over the dead languages, is it possible to deduce even all living languages from one primitive speech?

Even those who believe in a primitive language admit that the three families of language are irreducible, *i.e.* incapable of being derived from one another.

"These three systems of grammar (Arian, Semitic, and Turanian), are," says Professor Max Müller, "*perfectly distinct, and it is impossible to derive the grammatical forms of the one from those of the other*, though we cannot deny that in their radical elements the three families of human speech may have had a common source."

Attempts have, indeed, been made to connect Hebrew and Sanskrit, but the adduced points of osculation are so few and dubious, that such attempts must be pronounced to be egregious failures. Dr. Prichard endeavoured to prove a connection between Celtic and Hebrew, but " he succeeds no better than those who had made the same attempt before him. In nearly every case, the identity of the terms compared is questionable, and in many it is demonstrably imaginary."*

It must then be allowed, that the Indo-European and Semitic families are in their grammatical system (which affords the truest, if not the only test of affinity) radically distinct, and can in no way be derived from each other. The motto of the old school, that "all languages are dialects of a single one," must be abandoned for ever.

But even if it could be shown that there is an affinity between Hebrew and Sanskrit, a far more difficult task would remain for those who endeavour to prove from philology the original unity of the human race; for it would be still necessary for them to show further the Turanian unity, and the possibility of a primitive nucleus, not only for Semitic, and Arian, and Turanian languages, (assuming this to comprise even the Malay,

---

* Garnett's *Philol. Essays*, p. 85, &c., where the supposed instances are examined. Most of them are, as might have been expected, simple onomatopœias of the most obvious kind. See Renan, *Hist. des Langues Sém.* p. 450 seqq. Nothing requires more care than an inquiry of this kind;—often two words which have identically the same letters have no connection with each other, while two others derived from a common source have not one letter in common. As an instance of the former case, take the French *souris* "a smile," and *souris* "a mouse," (from *subridere* and *sorex* respectively); as an instance of the latter, take the word cousin, derived from *soror* through *consobrinus*.

Australian, Papuan, Kaffir, Esquimaux, &c.), but also for these languages and the ungrammatical, unagglutinative, monosyllabic Chinese. Yet, such is the task undertaken, with vast learning and marvellous ingenuity, by Professor Müller and Baron Bunsen. It will, however, be admitted, that the proved existence of great irreducible families is a strong *à priori* evidence against them. Let us examine some of their main arguments.

1. "Though in physical ethnology we cannot derive the Negro from the Malay, or the Malay from the Negro type, we may look upon each as a modification of a common and more general type. The same applies to the types of language. We cannot derive Sanskrit from Hebrew, or Hebrew from Sanskrit: but we can well understand how both may have proceeded from one common source."[*]

Thus it is argued, that although these families of language cannot, in their present state, have been derived from each other, yet it is possible to suppose that they are widely diverging radii from the same original centre; that they may all have sprung from a primitive language, whose existence we may conjecture, just as we should

* *Outlines,* i. 476.

have conjectured the existence of such a language as the Latin, to account for the numerous
marks of affinity between the Romance dialects.

But this proposition is hedged in by difficulties.
The very unity of the great Arian and Semitic
families tells powerfully against it.   If the
members of these families retain, after the
separation of many hundred years, the most
striking similarity, in the roots of the words
which refer to the relations of life, and to the
primitive acts of weaving and the working of
metals, how is it possible to believe that the
points of resemblance between Sanskrit and
Hebrew, or between Chinese and Greek, are so
extremely few, and so dubiously vague, that they
hardly afford the shadow of a presumption in
favour of the hypothesis which they are adduced
to support ?   Even if we grant the postulated
length of time—thousands and thousands of
years—which take us back to a period when
historical "chronology borders on the geologic
eras," which will alone render such a diversity of
sister languages *possible*, we confess that it still
appears to us so improbable, that it rather wears
the appearance of an arbitrary hypothesis, than
an inductive conclusion.

2. The main affinities supposed to exist be-

tween language of the different families, will be
found at large in the " Outlines of the Philosophy
of Universal History." Great stress is there laid
(i.) on the supposed discovery of certain non-Sans-
kritic elements in Celtic, which form the link by
which the Indo-European family approaches the
Turanian formations; and (ii.) the establishment
of a connection between the Arian and Semitic
families, by a reduction of the Hebrew triliteral
roots to biliteral ones.

(i.) While wishing to allow the fullest weight to
everything which has been adduced by Dr. Meyer
in proof of this discovery, and not professing to
be fully able to weigh the value of the evidence,
we cannot think that his researches have at all
settled the question. Beyond certain accidental
and vague resemblances, a few lexicographical
similarities* easily explicable by onomatopœia, and
a few words † adopted in consequence of foreign

---

* *Outlines*, i. 143, 165 seqq.

† A very curious instance of this is the word ‎שירן‎ *shoes*,
found in a Syro-Chaldaic Lectionarium in the Vatican. We may
here remark that Dr. Young's celebrated calculation—that, if eight
words are identical in two languages, the chances of a direct
relation between the languages are 100,000 to one—is very
exceptionable. See Dr. Latham, in the *Encycl. Brit.* Art. *Language*. The greatest care is necessary to distinguish between
words really cognate, and accidental isolated resemblances. See
Pictet, *Orig. Ind.* p. 13, 17.

P

influences, and that general affinity which we
should expect from the ascertained fact of the
psychological unity of the human race, nothing
that we have hitherto met with seems at all
adequate to counterbalance the enormous difficulty of supposing that families, closely united
together, yet radically distinct from each other,
could, even during thousands of years, have
diverged so widely from a common source.
Again, we must ask, if it was possible for one
primitive language to pass through stages of
development so irreconcileably different as those
represented by Hebrew and Sanskrit, what cause
can be adduced sufficient to account for the fact
that after the lapse of three millenniums, a Lithu-
anian peasant could almost understand the com-
monest of Sanskrit verbs ?*

The Chinese must always remain a stumbling-
block in the way of all theories respecting a
primitive language. Radical as is the dissimi-
larity between Arian and Semitic languages, and
wide as is the abyss between their grammatical
systems, yet they almost appear like sisters when
compared with the Chinese, which has nothing
like the organic principle of grammar at all.
Indeed, so wide is the difference between Chinese

* *Survey of Lang.* p. 11.

and Sanskrit, that the richness of human intelligence in the formation of language receives no more striking illustration than the fact that, as we have already observed, these languages have absolutely *nothing* in common except the end at which they aim. This end is in both cases the expression of thought, and it is attained as well in Chinese as in the grammatical languages, although the means are wholly different.

(ii.) Very great stress has been laid on the general lexicographical affinity between Hebrew and Sanskrit, produced by the reduction of the Hebrew triliteral roots to biliteral ones. This was suggested by Klaproth, and supported with great learning and industry by Fürst and Delitzsch. We have already alluded to it, and can only repeat here, that it is not accepted as certain, or even as probable, by some high authorities. We cannot now recount the numerous and weighty objections brought against this attempt by the historian of the Semitic languages*.—objections derived mainly from the extreme laxity of the process which even involves the extraordinary hypothesis, that these triliteral roots were formed by prefixes and suffixes, and that the prefixes have nothing determinate about them,

---

* Renan, p. 216.

P 2

but that every letter in the alphabet might be used
for the purpose,—an hypothesis contrary to the
most essential principles of language.   It will be
sufficient to repeat his questions.   How can we
conceive the passage from the monosyllabic to
the triliteral stage ?   What cause can be assigned
for it ?   At what epoch did it take place ?   Was
it due to the multiplication of ideas or the invention of writing ?   Was this stage of grammatical
innovation the result of chance, or of a common
agreement ?   To these inquiries, no answer ever
has been or can be given.   The supposition
of an original biliteralism must be considered
(as we said before) simply as a convenient hypothesis, and must not be taken for an historical
fact.

Languages, of course, develope ; but it is, as
we have seen, by the germinal development of a
rudimentary idea, and not by this process of gross
exterior concretion for which no single parallel
can be suggested.   The only monosyllabic dialects which we know, viz., those of Eastern Asia,
have continued monosyllabic for unknown ages.
Chinese cannot attain to a grammar, and the
Semitic languages could never arrive either at
regularly written vowels, or at a satisfactory
system of moods and tenses.   Grammar is to a

language its *unalterable* individuality. The growth and change of language has nothing analogous to grammatical revolution; it is due to a silent, a spontaneous, an unconscious genius, not to deliberate reflexion, or conscious alteration. All idioms which have been artificially altered (*e.g.* Rabbinic Hebrew), betray the fact by their harshness and awkwardness,—their want of harmony and flexibility; they bear no resemblance to those languages which are the genuine instrument of a nation's thoughts.

3. Undoubtedly the strongest argument in favour of a Primitive Language arises from the phenomenon of several languages which appear to occupy an anomalous position on the frontier of the great kingdoms of speech, and to present a lexicographical affinity with one family, and a grammatical affinity with another family. Such languages are the Egyptian, the Berber, the Touareg, and generally the languages of Northern and Eastern Africa, which resemble the Semitic tongues, in some parts of their vocabulary, but differ widely from them in all the rest. Similarly, the Tibetian and Burmese stand on the confines of the monosyllabic languages.

Perhaps the only way to account for these strange appearances is to suppose that language had a period of primitive *fusibility*,* during which they were susceptible of great modification from contact with other languages also in an ante-historical and embryonary state. It is impossible, otherwise, to explain the identity, for instance, of the pronouns and numerals in Coptic and the Semitic languages, or to account for the fact that among different races *t* is the sign of the second person singular, and *n*, of the first person plural. The analogies which guided the first men in such cases entirely escape our power of perception. Philology in its present state has not sufficient materials to decide how can it be that a few essential elements in a vocabulary should be nearly the same in two languages, while yet they differ totally in so important a particular as the flexions of the noun and verb. We know, however, as an historical fact, that wide as is the difference between the Semitic and Egyptian systems of civilisation, and different as are the physical traits of the two nations, yet that for many ages the Semitic influence was very strongly felt in Egypt.† Egypt, indeed, was only a narrow valley, surrounded by Semitic Nomads, who lived side

---

* *Hist. des Langues Sém.* p. 84 seqq.
† Renan quotes Mövers, *Die Phœnizien,* i. 33.

by side with the sedentary population; some-times victorious, sometimes subject,—always detested. The Egyptian language belongs then to a Chamitic family, to which also belong the Ber-ber, and other indigenous languages of Northern Africa; a family which is spread in Africa from the Red Sea to Senegal, and from the Mediter-ranean to the Niger.

Of these languages, the Berber presents nume-rous grammatical affinities with the Hebrew, but is completely distinct in its vocabulary. This, too, may be accounted for by the fact, that it has also been submitted to long ages of Semitic influ-ence, in consequence of its relations with Cartha-ginian and Arabic. The possibility of a state of language so incomplete as to admit of these radical influences from contact with superior idioms, is an important subject for philological inquiry.

We are forced then to conclude that whatever may be the other arguments, physiological and historical, for a material unity of the human race, a belief, which understood in a high psychological sense, will meet with universal acceptation, philo-logy alone, so far as it has yet proceeded, adds no contribution to the probability of such a view. Of the primitive men we know little or nothing, nor can we advance beyond the region of con-

jecture; but language *does* reveal to us something about the origin of *nations*, and the apparition of the main *races* of humanity would
appear to have been in the following succession.

' 1st. Inferior races which have no history,
covering the soil since an epoch which must be
determined by geology rather than by history.*
In general, these races have disappeared in those
parts of the world where the great civilised races
have advanced. The Arians and the Semites have
everywhere found the traces of these half-savage
tribes which they exterminate, and which often
survive in their legends as gigantic or magical,
and autochthonous races.   The relics of their
primitive humanity are found in those parts of
the world where the great races have not established themselves, and they present a profound
diversity, varying from the sweet and simple
child of the Antilles to the voluptuous Tahitian,
and the wicked population of Borneo and Assam.
But wherever found, these primitive tribes betray
an absolute incapacity for organisation and progress ; and they wither away before the advance
of civilisation, and pine into a sickness and

---

* *Hist. des Langues Sém.* 490, 491.   Whenever passages are in
semi-inverted commas, it will be understood that they are almost
directly translated from the author referred to.

decay from which, as far as we can see at present, not even the healing influences of Christianity are sufficient to rescue them.[*]

'2ndly. The apparition of the first civilised races; Chinese in Eastern Asia, the Cushites and Chamites in Western Asia and Africa. Early civilisations stamped with a materialistic character; religious and poetic instincts slightly developed; a feeble sentiment of art, but a refined sentiment of elegance; a great aptitude for manual arts and the applied sciences; literatures exact, but without an ideal; a turn for business, but an absence of public spirit and political life; perfect administrations, but little military aptitude; language monosyllabic and · flexionless (Egyptian, Chinese); hieroglyphic or ideographic systems of writing. These races have a history of three or four thousand years before the Christian era. All the Cushite and Chamite civilisations have disappeared before the advance of the Arians and Shemites; but in China this type of primitive civilisation has survived even to the present day.

'3rdly. Apparition of the great noble races,

[*] The accounts of various missionaries among the New Zealanders, American Indians, and aboriginal Australians, give a strange and *mournful* confirmation of these assertions.

Arians and Shemites, coming from the Imäus.
These races appeared simultaneously in history,
the Shemites in Armenia, the Arians in Bactriana,
about two thousand years before the Christian
era. Inferior to the Chamites and Cushites in
external civilisation, material works, and the
science of imperial organisation, they infinitely
excel them in vigour, courage, poetic and
religious genius. The Arians far surpass the
Shemites in political and military arts, and in
their intelligence and capacity for rational speculation, but the Shemites long preserved a religious
superiority, and ended by drawing almost every
Arian nation to their monotheistic conceptions.
In this point of view Islamism crowns the essential work of the Shemites, which has been to
simplify the human spirit—to banish polytheism
and those enormous complications in which the
religious thought of the Arians became entangled.
This mission once accomplished, the Shemite race
rapidly declines, and leaves the Arian race to
march alone at the head of the destinies of
mankind.'

Such are some of the conclusions to which
philology would seem to point; but they are
only stated with a perfect readiness to abandon
all present inferences when we are required to

do so by a wider knowledge, and with a profound
consciousness that what we know as yet is but
a drop compared to the ocean, which is still
untraversed and unknown.

NOTE.—For some very accurate original observations on the
Egyptian language, I refer the reader to a remarkable book, the
Genesis of the Earth and Man, 2nd. ed. pp. 255—263. To
Mr. Reginald Stuart Poole, the Editor of that candid and learned
Essay, I take this opportunity of returning my thanks.

CHAPTER XI.

THE FUTURE OF LANGUAGE.

" Even as a hawke fleeth not his with one wing, even so a man reacheth not to excellency with one tongue."—ROGER ASCHAM.

WE have seen that philology offers no proof of a universal primitive language. The question now arises, Is there any probability of a universal future language? Does it seem likely that the day will ever come when all men shall be of one speech? The noble Indo-Germanic race has carried its power and its conquests over a vast surface of the globe, and our own tongue *— which receives by common consent the meed of the most powerful of existing languages—is probably spoken by at least a hundred millions of the human race. Have we any reason to believe

---

* That there is more probability in favour of English becoming prevalent throughout the globe, than in favour of any other language acquiring a future universality, is admitted by all who have studied the subject. See Benloew, *Aperçu Général*, p. 92. Grimm, *Ueber der Ursprung*, p. 50. Russian is another language which probably has a great future.

that English will hereafter prevail over every
other dialect, and become in some form or other
the language of the world ?

That the Arian race is the destined inheritor
of the future world seems clear to the least
discriminating glance, because it has proved
itself to be the race most capable of perfectibility,
and therefore most worthy of power. But that
any one language spoken by the various branches
of their race will ultimately prevail to the ex-
clusion of all others is an event which hardly
seems probable; if probable, it is still in the
present state of the world undesirable; and even
were it certain, yet the permanent existence of
such a language is incompatible with the present
condition of human intelligence.

1. The development of a future universal language seems improbable. It is true that dialects
become merged in languages, and these languages
lost in others still more extensive, just as streams
flow into rivers, and rivers into the sea. It is
true that diversity of idioms is the characteristic
of barbarism, and unity the slow result of civilisation. But against these considerations we
must set the extraordinary tenacity of national
associations and national characteristics. However far we may look into the future, we see

nothing to show us that the distinctions of nations were not intended to be as permanent as the oceans that divide them; and nothing to make us expect that all humankind will be gathered hereafter (in its present general condition) under one universal empire, and into one school of religion and of thought.

2. But even were it probable that there would be only one language hereafter, such a consummation would not be desirable, because it would greatly hinder the search for truth, and would tend to reduce men to a dead level of uniformity, a Chinese dryness and mediocrity of intelligence. It is, indeed, conceivable that a universal growth of mammon-worship, making merchandise almost the only occupation of mankind, might tend to give to languages that form of practical abbreviation which we find in telegraphic despatches, and which, to economise phrases and expense, neglects grammar, and puts down the smallest possible number of words, with no desire beyond that of being barely understood.* But such abbreviation, useful as it may be for certain purposes, would, if applied to all the forms of language, despoil it for ever of all ornament and all poetic charm, and so far from enabling us to

* Benloew, *Aperçu Général*, p. 91.

rival the noble languages of antiquity, would reduce us to a condition from which the instincts of our race would inevitably break loose, to begin a fresh career of discovery and thought.

"Truths," said Coleridge,* "of all others the most awful and interesting are too often considered so true that they lose all the power of truth, and lie bed-ridden in the dormitory of the soul, side by side with the most depised and exploded errors." By frequent use, as by repeated attrition, the brightness and beauty of a word is worn bare, and it requires a distinct effort of attention to restore the full significance to the forms of expression with which we are most familiar. "Hence it is," says Mr. Mill,† "that the traditional maxims of old experience, though seldom questioned, have often so little effect on the conduct of life, because their meaning is never, by most persons, really felt, until personal experience has brought it home. And thus, also, it is that so many doctrines of religion, ethics, and even politics, so full of meaning and reality to first converts, have manifested a tendency to degenerate rapidly into lifeless dogmas, which tendency all the efforts of an education expressly and skilfully directed to

* *Aids to Reflection*, p. 1.   † Mill's *Logic*, ii. 221.

keeping the meaning alive are barely found sufficient to counteract." The weight and importance
of these remarks will best be felt by those who
have observed how new and rare meanings are
perceived when we read the words, for instance,
of Holy Writ in their original language, and
lose sight for a moment of those groundless
fancies with which long association has confused
our perception. To study the Bible in other
languages than our own is like looking upon the
Urim and Thummim when, for him who rightly
consulted it, the fire of the divine messages
flashed upon its oracular and graven gems.

Hence language is most important, is almost
indispensable to the human race for the perpetual
preservation of truths which would otherwise be
banished "to the lumber-room of the memory,"
rather than be prepared for use "in the work-
shop of the mind." For words are constantly
acquiring new shades of meaning in consequence
of the things which they connote, and to such an
extent is this the case, that our quotations of an
author's actual words often involve a gross
anachronism, because his "pure ideas" * have

* These thoughts are admirably developed in a beautiful Essay
on the Abstract Idea of the New Testament, by Mr. Jowett (ii. 90).
See, too, W. von Humboldt's tract *Ueber d. Entstehen d. grammat.*

often become our "mixed modes." If, for instance, we were to use the word "gravitation" in translating various passages of ancient authors, we might be led to assert that the great discovery of Newton had been anticipated by hundreds of years; and yet we know that those authors had no conception whatever of the law which that word recalls to our minds.

Both in the history of the world, and in the growth of individual intellects, the study of language has produced the noblest results. To it more than to any other cause we owe the outburst of freedom in thought which produced the Reformation, and the mighty advance of humanity which followed that emancipation of the intellect of Europe from the ignorance fostered by a depressing superstition; and to it in very great measure we owe the matchless power and beauty of our own tongue. "Indeed, the adoption of words from dead languages into English has, above all other causes, tended to increase the number of our simple ideas, because the associations of such words being lost in the transfer

Formen und ihren Einfluss auf die Ideenentwickelung, as well as the chapter *Ueber die Verschiedenheit des Menschlichen Sprachbaues,* which forms the introduction to the treatise on the Kawi language.

they are at once refined from all alloy of sense
and experience."

The old Roman poet,* proud in the unusual
erudition which had made him master of three
languages, used to declare, that he had three
hearts, and his opinion has been echoed by a
modern poet †·with emphatic commendation—

> " Mit jeder Sprache mehr, die Du erlernst, befreist
> Du einen bis daher in Dir gebundenen Geist,
> Der jetzo thätig wird mit eigner Deukverbindung,
> Die aufschliesst unbekannt gewesene Weltempfindung.
> Ein alter Dichter, der nur dreier Sprachen Gaben
> Besessen, rühmte sich der Seelen drei zu haben,
> Und wirklich hätt' in sich alle Menschengeister
> Der Geist vereint, der recht wür' alle Sprachen Meister."

The Emperor Charles V. went still further, and
declared that " in proportion ‡ to the number of
languages which a man knew, in that proportion
was he more of a man." There may have been
exaggeration in this expression, but at any rate
it arose from the conviction of an important
truth. And we may add with Göthe the un-

` * Q. Ennius tria corda se habere dicebat, quod loqui Græce et
Latine et Osce sciret."—A. Gell.

† Rückert.

‡ "Il disoit et répétoit souvent, quand il tomboit sur la beauté
des langues, ... qu'autant de langues que l'homme sçait parler,
autant de fois est il homme."—Brantome.

doubted certainty, "Wer fremde sprache nicht kennt, weiss nichts von seiner eigenen." Perhaps in this sentence we may find the reasons why so few know their own language in half its richness and power.

3. A universal language could not, in the present state of human intelligence, last for any long period. New circumstances of life, new discoveries of thought, new conquests of art and science, would require new forms of expression. The influences of climate and history would produce fresh revolutions in the character of nations, and the change of character would necessitate modifications of the prevalent idiom, which in the course of time would diverge so widely from the parent language, as to be unintelligible unless separately acquired. There is in language, as we have seen repeatedly, an organic life; it is an incessant act of creation, ever progressing, ever developing. To reduce it to one stereotyped * and universal form would be to contradict the very law of its being, by substituting an eternal immobility for that power of growth and alteration which constitutes its very existence.

If all men be hereafter of one speech, it can

* See Destutt de Tracy, *Grammaire Or.* vi.

only be after they have arrived at a condition when knowledge has superseded the necessity of inquiry, when intuition supplies the place of discovery, and certainty has been substituted for faith. As far as the science of philology can pronounce an opinion, we must infer, that the familiar line will remain true henceforth as heretofore—

Πολλαὶ μὲν Θνητοῖς γλῶτται, μία' δ' Ἀθανάτοισι.
Mortals have many languages, the Immortals one alone.

APPENDIX.

A LIST OF SOME BOOKS, VALUABLE AS AIDS IN
THE GENERAL STUDY OF PHILOLOGY.

GERMAN.

Bopp, Vergleichende Grammatik.
Bopp, Vokalismus.
Bopp, Accentuationssystem.
Grimm, Ueber den Ursprung der Sprache. Berlin, 1858.
Grimm, Geschichte der Deutsch. Sprache.
Grimm, Ueber die namen der Donners. 1856.
Heyse, System der Sprachwissenschaft. Berlin, 1856.
Steinthal, Der Ursprung der Sprache. Berlin, 1858.
W. von Humboldt, Ueber die Verschiedenheit des Menschlichen
    Sprachbaues. 1836.
Steinthal, Grammatik, Logik, und Psychologie. Berlin, 1855.
Lersch, Die Sprachphilosophie der Alten. Bonn, 1841.
Weber, Indische Skizzen. Berlin, 1857.
Pott, Etymologische Forschungen.
Pott, Die Ungleichheit Menschlicher Rassen.
Schlegel, Philosophische Vorlesungen. Wien. 1830.
Schleicher, Linguist. Untersuchungen.
Zeuss, Grammatica Keltica.

FRENCH.

Renan, De l'Origine du Langage. 2me ed. Paris, 1858.
Renan, Histoire et Système Comparés des Langues Sémitiques.
    Paris, 1858.
Benloew, Aperçu Général de la Science Comparative des Lan-
    gues. Paris, 1858.

Benloew, De l'Accentuation dans les langues Indo-Européennes.
Paris, 1847.
Charma, Essai sur le Langage. Paris, 1846.
Pictet, Les Origines Indo-Européennes. Paris, 1859.
Nodier, Notions de Linguistique.
Victor Cousin, Cours de 1829, et Fragmens Philosophiques.
Degerando, De signes et de l'art de penser.
Balbi, Introduction à l'atlas ethnographique du globe.
Fauriel, Dante et les Origines de la Langue et de la Littérature
Italienne.
Thommerel, Sur la Fusion de l'Anglo-Norman avec l'Anglo-
Saxon.

ENGLISH.

Horne Tooke, Diversions of Purley.
Harris, Hermes.
Bunsen, Philosophy of Universal History.
Max Müller, Survey of Languages.
Max Müller, Oxford Essay on Comparative Mythology.
Latham, The English Language.
Dr. Donaldson, New Cratylus.
Dr. Donaldson, Varronianus.
Garnett, Philosophical Essays.
Hensleigh Wedgwood, Etymological Dictionary.
Transactions of the Philological Society.

I have here indicated a few only out of a very
large number of books which will be found useful
by a Philological student. The list might be very
easily and very considerably enlarged, but any
one who once takes up the study will find in the
books here mentioned ample materials on which
to commence. The questions suggested by the

study of Language are so closely connected with those of Moral Philosophy, that almost every philosophical work contains matter valuable to the Philologist. From Plato, Aristotle, and Cicero, down to Locke and Leibnitz, there is no great philosopher who has not in some degree entered on reasonings respecting the nature and origin of Language. Perhaps there is no more important result from the study of Language than the greater clearness which it necessarily gives to our metaphysical conceptions, and the attention which it necessarily turns to the phenomena of the mind.

THE END.

BRADBURY AND EVANS, PRINTERS, WHITEFRIARS.